Elance

by Karen Lacey

ALPHA

A member of Penguin Group (USA) Inc.

For my father.

ALPHA BOOKS

Published by Penguin Group (USA) Inc.

Penguin Group (USA) Inc., 375 Hudson Street, New York, New York 10014, USA • Penguin Group (Canada), 90 Eglinton Avenue East, Suite 700, Toronto, Ontario M4P 2Y3, Canada (a division of Pearson Penguin Canada Inc.) • Penguin Books Ltd., 80 Strand, London WC2R 0RL, England • Penguin Ireland, 25 St. Stephen's Green, Dublin 2, Ireland (a division of Penguin Books Ltd.) • Penguin Group (Australia), 250 Camberwell Road, Camberwell, Victoria 3124, Australia (a division of Pearson Australia Group Pty. Ltd.) • Penguin Books India Pvt. Ltd., 11 Community Centre, Panchsheel Park, New Delhi—110 017, India • Penguin Group (NZ), 67 Apollo Drive, Rosedale, North Shore, Auckland 1311, New Zealand (a division of Pearson New Zealand Ltd.) • Penguin Books (South Africa) (Pty.) Ltd., 24 Sturdee Avenue, Rosebank, Johannesburg 2196, South Africa • Penguin Books Ltd., Registered Offices: 80 Strand, London WC2R 0RL, England

Copyright © 2012 by Karen Lacey

International Standard Book Number: 978-1-61564-207-6
Library of Congress Catalog Card Number: 2012933509

14   13   12   8   7   6   5   4   3   2   1

Interpretation of the printing code: The rightmost number of the first series of numbers is the year of the book's printing; the rightmost number of the second series of numbers is the number of the book's printing. For example, a printing code of 12-1 shows that the first printing occurred in 2012.

Printed in the United States of America

Most Alpha books are available at special quantity discounts for bulk purchases for sales promotions, premiums, fund-raising, or educational use. Special books, or book excerpts, can also be created to fit specific needs. For details, write: Special Markets, Alpha Books, 375 Hudson Street, New York, NY 10014.

Publisher: *Mike Sanders*
Executive Managing Editor: *Billy Fields*
Executive Acquisitions Editor: *Lori Cates Hand*
Development Editor: *Mark Reddin*
Senior Production Editor: *Kayla Dugger*
Copy Editor: *Louise Lund*

Cover Designer: *Rebecca Batchelor*
Book Designers: *William Thomas, Rebecca Batchelor*
Indexer: *Johnna VanHoose Dinse*
Layout: *Brian Massey*
Proofreader: *John Etchison*

Contents

Introduction

My goal with this book is to help you achieve the success with Elance that I've had. Through the online work world, I've been able to go places and achieve personal goals I never imagined I could. Once I got started, the avenues of opportunity just seemed to keep expanding. I know you can experience this, too, and I wish I'd had this kind of go-to resource when I first started.

My story began in early 2008, when I found myself jobless, with a bank account close to empty, and no options in sight. I'd given up my lucrative, six-figure position with an international financial services firm—including the security, full benefits, and matching 401(k)—and had instead chosen the freedom, travel, and happiness I believed were within reach of an independent contractor. However, each business plan I devised to replace my income became waterlogged by the rising global recession.

Then one rainy day in Southern California, I stumbled upon the world of online freelancing. They say that when one door slams shut, another one opens. However true that may be, a door certainly did open for me—one named Elance.com. I grabbed my laptop, hoisted up my 6-pound stray cat named Behemoth, and stepped through, never to look back.

I tried other online work sites and achieved success on some. But Elance stood above the others in quality of jobs and ease of use. It's because of this that I chose to write a book about this website. My ghostwriting, editing, and proofreading business through Elance led to ghostwriting seven books, one of which won second place in a national contest. I have edited and proofread countless others and became editor-in-chief for an active website promoting a variety of political views.

More importantly, I pulled myself away from what I perceived as a brutish path of soul-hardening corporate life and built a successful freelance business. I now have a wealth of experience and advice to help you achieve the same level of freedom I have, whether as a business owner or freelancer.

I have been both a client and a contractor for Elance and in the process have been able to live and work in Buenos Aires, Argentina, and in Cocoa Beach, Florida, with its endless white sand beaches. I am currently writing this from Palm Desert, California, all the while traveling with my tiny black cat and a promise to myself never to dread another Monday morning. My cat and my dream are thriving.

Your dreams can thrive, too. Don't just read the book and then set it down; take action along the way. Open your Elance account, get those first projects going, and begin building your dream life step-by-step. If I can do it, you certainly can, too. You'll find advice in this book not only from me, but from other successful Elance contractors and clients. Learn from the best, and apply what works for your situation and personality.

Read on, and good luck!

How This Book Is Organized

The Complete Idiot's Guide to Elance is divided into four major parts.

Part 1, The New Way of Doing Business, begins by exploring the phenomenal boom in the online work world for both contractors and clients. Working online gives people time to step back and design their professional images to represent their business in the most constructive light possible. These and other advantages individuals and businesses have discovered on Elance are covered, as well as the basic steps to open an Elance account (either to hire or be hired). By the end of this part, you'll be up and running on Elance.

Part 2, Selling Your Services as an Elance Contractor, is devoted to contractors, but Elance clients will be well served to read it, too. Understanding the freelancers' world is helpful in finding and hiring the most appropriate people for your projects. The contractor will learn how to design a profile and online image to help attract the best clients, as well as how to write detailed proposals for winning the jobs of their choosing. I also cover how to utilize the Elance platform to manage jobs easily and effectively and how to develop a real connection with the client. This in turn will help bring in repeat business and referrals. This part ends with a chapter devoted to the new Elance contractor, detailing ways to help get started quickly, and how to build a positive online reputation.

Part 3, Growing Your Business as an Elance Client, is devoted to Elance clients looking to hire the best talent possible. However, contractors should read this part, too, so they understand what the client is looking for and what their Elance experience is like. The client will learn how they are actually competing for the best contractors and therefore how to attract this talent. I discuss how to identify suitable contractors by studying their profiles, track records, and portfolios of sample work. Then I cover how to write clear and attractive job posts so the right freelancers bid on your project. I also provide best practices for how to proactively manage your jobs and freelancers and create ongoing relationships. This part concludes with a chapter devoted to how the Elance platform enables the online work experience and how the widgets, gadgets, and add-ons all serve to make sure that the virtual office runs smoothly.

Part 4, Advanced Elancing for Contractors and Clients, covers some of the more detailed areas of the Elance virtual work platform for both contractors and clients. Elance doesn't just serve to introduce the two, but also provides a safe and effective work environment. Project agreements, Terms of Service, and contractor and client online safety are reviewed. I also give in-depth instructions on how to fine-tune account settings. Many contractors and clients alike don't realize the full list of opportunities at the end of jobs, including repeat business and referrals. I discuss these as well as include a trouble-shooting guide for what to do if you end up with an unproductive business relationship. It doesn't happen often, but it's best to know what to do if it does. The part finishes with a chapter on the Elance community. Advice, help, and camaraderie exist amongst Elancers, and I'll show you how to get involved.

The Complete Idiot's Guide to Elance also includes a glossary of Elance and virtual work world terms. In addition, I include an appendix with several sample contractor proposals and client job posts to help both sides refine these important avenues of communication.

Extras

As you read through the book, you'll notice sidebars that contain definitions, tips, warnings, and miscellaneous information to help you better understand Elance.

DEFINITION

Check these sidebars for common terms used within Elance and the virtual work world.

TOP TIPS

Secrets shared from the top contractors.

CYBER SNAGS

Here, you'll be alerted to common mistakes made in the online work world and how to avoid them.

BEST PRACTICES

Clients reveal their best practices in growing their business through Elance.

Acknowledgments

First and foremost, I want to thank my agent, Marilyn Allen, for sticking with me and believing in me long enough so we could finally get this project completed. Thank you! Lori Cates Hand, Mark Reddin, and Kayla Dugger, my editors from Penguin, thank you for your gentle, competent guidance.

At Elance, thank you so much, Carrie Stuart. You're a wonderful go-to person, solution finder, and problem un-sticker. Thank you also to Elance's CEO, Fabio Rosati, for taking the time to share your vision with me and to make sure I got the help I needed. Also thanks to York Poon, Jen Hansen, and Keith Do at Elance. Thank you to the brilliant and talented Elance contractors and clients who took the time to share their experience, insight, and wisdom with me. Hire these folks, work for them—they're the best!

But most of all, thank you to my father. Without your support ... who knows where I would be.

Special Thanks to the Technical Reviewers

The Complete Idiot's Guide to Elance was reviewed by experts who double-checked the accuracy of what you'll learn here, to help us ensure that this book gives you everything you need to know about Elance. Special thanks are extended to Carrie Stuart, Melissa Tilney, York Poon, Hyun Lee, and Jen Hansen.

Trademarks

All terms mentioned in this book that are known to be or are suspected of being trademarks or service marks have been appropriately capitalized. Alpha Books and Penguin Group (USA) Inc. cannot attest to the accuracy of this information. Use of a term in this book should not be regarded as affecting the validity of any trademark or service mark.

The New Way of Doing Business

1

These first two chapters explore the phenomenal boom in the online work world for both contractors and clients. Working online gives people time to step back and design their professional image to represent their business in the most constructive light possible. I discuss these and other advantages individuals and businesses have discovered on Elance and what keeps them coming back for more.

Also, I go through the basic steps to open an Elance account either to hire or be hired. By the end of this part, you'll be up and running on Elance.

Welcome to the Twenty-First Century

In This Chapter

- Learning basic Elance terms
- How the independent contractor role is increasing
- Real stories from the field
- Key benefits to building your business online
- A successful freelancer's work habits

Hiring and working online isn't nearly as difficult or as fraught with internet dangers as people think. In fact, data shows this truly is the new twenty-first-century way of doing business. Buying books on Amazon and music through iTunes is the new normal. Soon, finding work or growing your business online will be, too.

As the work world flattens, it'll be less and less unusual for an online receptionist to "show up" for work from 2,000 miles away. And more morning commutes will consist of making coffee, having breakfast with the kids, and turning on the laptop rather than sitting for hours in congested traffic.

As with so many technological advances, at first it may seem intimidating, but as you learn and gain experience you will discover advantages you never knew existed. Virtual commuting is here to stay. Have a look and you just might be pleasantly surprised.

Going Virtual

The trends highlighting the virtual work world are astounding. While the world economy remains restless and unsure at best, online work has exploded. They say that within every slump something will be growing somewhere—you just need to look closely. Okay, let's look.

In 2011, Elance alone saw its online hiring grow by more than 100 percent. Over 650,000 new jobs were posted, and membership grew by over 120 percent. These numbers are no blip on the screen of the dying. They underscore a dynamic global trend. Something's going on here!

More than 1.3 million people are registered on Elance and over 17,000 new contractors join every week. In an Elance survey, 87 percent of independent business owners said that hiring contractors online was a "vital" part of business for them. Eighty-three percent said over the next 12 months they plan to hire one half or more of their workers online.

This is not simply a matter of U.S. companies rushing overseas to hire cheap labor. American workers are seeing a huge boon in finding jobs online. In 2011, U.S.-based contractors provided services in over 140 countries around the globe. The hiring of American workers increased from the previous year in over 60 of these countries. U.S. contractors and clients are still the largest group of Elance members.

BEST PRACTICES

Many business owners are hiring online for the cost savings. By hiring independent contractors, they don't have to supply office space, unemployment insurance, or health benefits. In today's world, these alone are huge savings.

Maybe you're thinking, "Nah, this is just for young folks who understand computers." Certainly the younger generations are catching on fast; they often do with technology. But many people of baby boomer age are freelancing and running their businesses with online hires.

Those riding on the virtual work world wave aren't from an isolated geographic or socioeconomic region, or of any distinct age or race. They are simply people who have seen and grasped this astounding opportunity. Read on!

Introduction to Elance Terms

Throughout this book I'll be using certain terms and expressions regularly. I'll list some of the most common ones here, but these and more will also appear in the glossary.

Contractors. Independent individuals and businesses that provide services on Elance. These are the folks that get hired. I also refer to them as freelancers.

Freelancers. Used interchangeably with contractors, these are the people who use Elance to find work.

Clients. Individuals or businesses that post jobs and hire contractors through Elance.

Bid. Much like on eBay, contractors place a dollar bid on jobs posted by clients. The client does not have to take, and doesn't always want to take, the lowest bid. Rather, she awards the job to the contractor of her choice.

Job post. Each client will create a job post on the Elance system. The post will describe in detail the work that needs to be done. Interested contractors then place bids on these postings. This is also known as a project posting.

Awarding a Job. When a client chooses the contractor she wants to hire, she awards the job to him. The contractor is then hired and the Elance virtual office infrastructure and features can be utilized.

Proposal. When a contractor places a bid on a job, he will include a written proposal explaining his terms and why he is the best choice for the job.

Profile. Each contractor creates a profile that prospective clients view to help determine if they're the best fit for their job. Clients also build profiles, but they're more limited in scope.

Category. Elance separates contractors into different categories depending on the services they provide. For example, a contractor may be in IT & Programming, or in Writing & Translation. Clients post their jobs within these categories.

Connects. A virtual currency used by Elance. You "pay" a certain number of Connects each time you submit a proposal. Each Elance membership plan comes with a monthly allocation of Connects. Paid membership plans allow members to add additional Connects at any time.

Cloud. Because Elance files, data, applications, and programs are managed and stored on the internet, business is considered to be conducted in the cloud.

The Freelancer Explosion

Individuals from all over the world have discovered the benefits of becoming an independent contractor. The modern structure of business has helped fuel this evolution. Gone are the days of working for a single company for your entire life and then retiring with a healthy pension.

TOP TIPS

Many successful contractors say getting laid off from their job was the best thing that could have happened to them, although they didn't realize it at the time. Through this unexpected change, they were able to start new careers and build lives that better suited their families and dreams.

Layoffs, relocations, and switching companies and careers have become the new way of doing business. Within this insecurity, however, has also risen opportunity. As employers search for a new kind of employee, workers are learning to redesign their lives in positive ways.

Freelancers of all kinds are flourishing with the opportunities that technology and the new work structure have provided. All of our lives are impacted by what we can do online, and this trend is also impacting the way we do business. The work world is evolving right before our eyes.

A New Kind of Freedom

The benefits to freelancing online are myriad. In a survey conducted by Elance, several key ones appeared:

- Control over your own schedule. No more fitting your life and personality into someone else's timetable.

- Being your own boss. Interestingly, for some this gave them a better feeling of job security because they weren't worried about getting laid off.

- The ability to follow your passion. Elance is full of success stories about people who were finally able to do what they loved for money, rather than what they had to do for money.

- No commute. No longer are you wasting hours and days of your life stuck in traffic.

- More choice over the projects you can do. You bid on only those jobs that appeal to you.

- No dress code. If jammies and slippers are your thing, no one's there to stop you.

- No cubicles. This outward manifestation of an inner sense of drone-ness is now passé.

Not surprisingly, given these advantages, many freelancers claim they're happier than ever in their new lives (see Figure 1.1). They look in life's rearview mirror and wonder how they ever lived any other way.

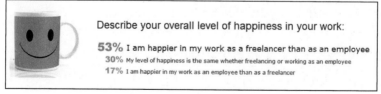

Describe your overall level of happiness in your work:

53% I am happier in my work as a freelancer than as an employee

30% My level of happiness is the same whether freelancing or working as an employee

17% I am happier in my work as an employee than as a freelancer

Figure 1.1: *In general, freelancers love their lifestyle.*

Full Time, Part Time, Nap Time

Freelancing doesn't need to be an all-or-nothing deal. How you go about building your business as a contractor is one more element that's totally up to you. No rule exists as to how fast or how slowly you should grow.

> **CYBER SNAGS**
>
> If you want to just test the freelancing water by dipping a toe in, remember that the beginning is the hardest. It takes time to build up the feedback and ratings to get the best jobs. So give it a try, by all means, but don't forget that it gets easier with time.

If you've recently been laid off and have all the time in the world, perhaps you can really launch yourself into this new endeavor. Even if you're still sending out traditional resumes, you can build your Elance profile and begin submitting bids and proposals.

Maybe you have full-time employment, but you also have a dream job you'd like to explore. In this case you wouldn't have the time to devote yourself entirely to freelancing. Going slow and gradually building up clients would work perfectly.

A rapidly expanding source of freelancers is the stay-at-home parent. Moms and dads alike, while looking after the kids, simultaneously crave the intellectual stimulus and adult interaction of work. Elance and freelancing dovetail into this situation nicely.

Projects can be completed while the kids nap or are away at school, or in the evening when the house has finally fallen quiet—whatever time suits your situation and personality. This is part of the magic of being an independent contractor.

Three Kids and a Kitchen Table

One example of the power of this new way of doing business comes from Melissa Johnson in Ohio. Melissa had been earning a cozy income in her corporate job when she became pregnant with her third child. A 4-year-old and a 2-year-old were a handful, but when a third baby appeared on the horizon, Melissa realized she needed to make a change. A friend of her husband suggested she look into Elance. According to Melissa, she spent five minutes checking it out and was hooked.

By placing bids and winning jobs, she began to build her knowledge of Elance and the freelancing life. But it wasn't until her third child was born that she took the leap; she quit her corporate job and devoted herself fully to raising her children and freelancing through Elance.

CYBER SNAGS

All top freelancers will tell you that carefully scheduling their work time is critical to success. It's far too easy to give in to life's demands and luxuries when not following a regular schedule.

Within four months of quitting her job, she built her freelancing business so she averaged more per month than at her corporate position, which paid $60,000 annually.

More importantly, and in her own words:

> "These days, instead of rushing myself and my children out the door at 7 A.M. only to sit in gridlock for an hour and then in a stuffy cubicle for another nine hours, I'm working from my home office, my couch, my kitchen table, or my patio. I'm leisurely taking my kids to and from preschool, nursing my infant during client calls, and getting dinner ready at a reasonable hour instead of hitting drive-thrus at 8 P.M."

Not everyone has enjoyed the success Melissa does, but her story shows not only what's possible but what's actually been accomplished.

The Online Opportunity for Businesses

Elance and the virtual work world function equally well for clients. Creating and running your own business is at the core of the entrepreneurial spirit. For many, their dream doesn't lie in the freelancer realm, but rather with building their business as quickly and efficiently as possible. Hiring contract workers to help them do this has proved priceless.

Starting a traditional brick-and-mortar business can entail hiring full-time staff, leasing property and equipment, and/or accruing various other overhead expenses. This alone prevents many from even attempting to start a new venture.

By utilizing online contractors, however, many of these issues simply don't exist. The ability to lower costs, and therefore have the ability and flexibility to start a new business, has meant that many goods and services are being produced that wouldn't be otherwise.

What's the Fuss About?

The advantages of hiring online are numerous. For just a start, look at these:

- The ability to scale up or down rapidly. You can choose to hire contractors on a project-by-project or hourly basis. If you need to pull back, hire fewer, if you want to expand, hire more.

- Experts are available for each job. You now have the entire world to choose from. If you are limited to only working with your in-house staff, you won't have the same wide range of talent.

- Faster project completion times. Contractors work project to project and usually won't have more than a few going at any one time. You get more of their time and attention. And if they can't get the project completed by the time you need it, you can hire someone else for that job.

- Robust information on contractors' prior work experience. With the feedback and ratings system, the online profile and portfolio, and the ability to communicate with your potential contractor, you have in-depth tools from which to hire.

- 24/7, 365-day-a-week access to talent.

- Often, contractors are less expensive to hire than full-time or onsite contractors, and extra benefits like health insurance and worker's compensation are eliminated. However, the key is to focus on the quality of the hire, not the expense.

BEST PRACTICES

Remember that despite the advantages of online hiring, it still takes time to make sensible choices when it comes down to awarding the job. Not all contractors on Elance will be the best choice for you. It's up to you to review the data available and make sound decisions.

The Story of Matthew Stibbe

To give you an idea of the kind of potential the online work world has for entrepreneurs, read the story of Matthew Stibbe, founder of London-based TurbineHQ.com.

In his own words:

> "I started TurbineHQ.com to simplify business paperwork. The idea is that companies sign up and their employees can do routine admin expenses claims, purchase requests, appraisals and time-off requests online. Nobody loves bureaucracy, but every business has to deal with this stuff and we're making it easier and faster.
>
> The whole thing, including the advertising, graphic design, marketing site and application, was done using Elance.com talent. It has let me build a very slick, professional application quickly and for a lot less money than I would have had to spend to do it the old-fashioned way. (I know because I used to run a 70+-person software company!) It's not just about saving money. Elance has helped me tap a much larger talent pool than I could reach in my local area. I've got people working for me in Ukraine, Vietnam, Argentina, and Romania.

Another more subtle benefit is that keeping overhead low has allowed me to build and launch the application while continuing to build my other business. Elance turns starting a new business into an 'and' situation rather than an 'either/or' situation. That's really quite magical. To put it another way, no Elance, no Turbine."

Matthew has gone on to hire out over 90 projects on Elance, has spent in excess of $50,000 on Elance freelancers, and has an ongoing project count of about a dozen.

Freelancing Is a Job

Many advantages exist to freelancing online, but it's still a job that requires discipline and hard work. In fact, it's this mandatory self-motivated infrastructure that causes so many to fail.

TOP TIPS

At the end of each work day, take 15 minutes to organize exactly what you'll be doing the next time you sit down to work. This way, as soon as you start another work session you'll know right where to go and what to do.

No one is going to check in on you to make sure you've met your goals. Most of the time, no one will be there to help you when you stumble or think you'll never make this silly idea work. (However, a robust Elance community does exist; see Chapter 18.)

Your schedule and goals are your own, and no one will be there to hold you accountable. For some people, this is no problem—in fact, they thrive in this environment. Others need a bit of structure or they tend to derail.

Consider how your personality fits into this spectrum. If you like to be held accountable, get a friend or family member to have you post your goals to them. Or design a set of rewards to go along with each goal reached.

For example, when you hit the 1,000-word mark, you can eat lunch, but not before. Or if you get your two proposals out today, you can watch the game tonight. Whatever it takes, but be aware of what you need to keep you going.

Hiring in the Cloud

People are people are people. As with contractors, just because you have all these advantages of hiring online doesn't mean there isn't a very real world out there with all kinds of people in it.

Elance works hard to ensure that the highest-quality freelancers are available—and they will be increasing these efforts in the future—but you must still do your due diligence.

Hiring in the cloud isn't that much different from hiring in person. You will pick winners and you will pick losers. In the cloud, you don't have to keep hiring the ones who don't meet your needs.

But great talent exists online, and if you follow the guidelines set forth in this book, you will be well on your way to success as a client.

When you find talented contractors, nurture the relationships, and hire them over and over again. This is how you begin to build your virtual team. To keep good-quality people, you must also be a good manager and leader. The Elance system is there to connect you with this talent and to enable the smooth flow of business.

The Least You Need to Know

- The virtual work world is one of the fastest-growing segments in the world.
- You're free to grow your freelancing business as quickly or as slowly as you like.
- Clients don't just save money; they also save time and potentially have fewer hassles along the way.
- Freelancing requires self-motivation and discipline.
- You might make a bad hiring choice on Elance, but you don't have to rehire them.

The Virtual You

In This Chapter

- Registering on Elance
- Making first impressions online
- Contractor qualities clients look for
- Learning from your competition
- Niche marketing considerations

Getting started on Elance is a fast and efficient process. The system is designed to streamline the enrollment stage so you're registered quickly and ready to do business. However, in order to succeed in the virtual work world, it's also crucial to take a step back and carefully consider your online persona. In this chapter, I cover both aspects.

In the ordinary world, you are assessed all the time by your physical appearance. What you project through your clothes, hairstyle, and overall appearance influences people; so does the way you speak, walk, and carry yourself. Strolling gracefully into a meeting wearing a tailored suit and holding a leather briefcase sends one message. Yet entering the same meeting dressed in shorts and flip flops and sporting beer tabs for earrings sends another.

Your online presence is no different, but too often contractors and clients forget that they're being judged from the first moment they "enter" the room. What you wear and whether or not you shaved won't be appraised. Rather, your new online image will take the place of you in person. You now have the opportunity to tailor this image exactly as you wish. This step is crucial to a successful online business and you must consider it early. Read on!

Registering on Elance

Let's start with getting up and running on Elance. It couldn't be easier. Creating an account is fast and within minutes you can be either a contractor or a client—or both.

Becoming a Client

It's absolutely free to join Elance as a client. Follow these steps to sign up:

1. On the Elance homepage (see Figure 2.1), click on **Post Your Job**. This will lead you into the one-page account setup process.

2. Fill out the online questionnaire where you'll create a password and user name. Elance guides you through this smoothly.

3. Verify your email address and you'll see a screen similar to Figure 2.2.

4. Congratulations, you're a member!

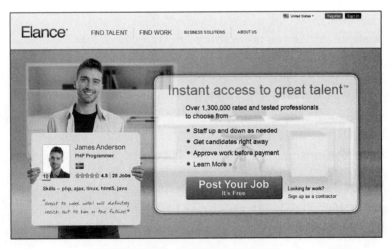

Figure 2.1: *The Elance homepage.*

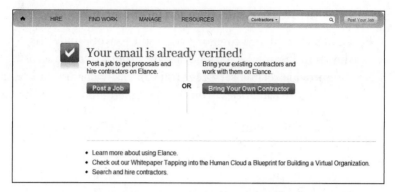

Figure 2.2: *Verifying your email address.*

Once you've verified your email address you can post a job (if you're a client). If you're itching to get started, be sure to read Part 3 of this book first. These tools and ideas will save you time and possibly money by helping you to get your job postings right while selecting the right contractor.

Some clients prefer to invite contractors they've previously worked with onto the Elance platform. In this case, you know who will be doing your project for you, and the Elance workrooms and escrow system provide a secure and efficient online environment. If this is your situation, simply click on the **Bring Your Own Contractor** button on the email verification screen and you will be guided through the process of inviting them to join.

Becoming a Contractor

Joining Elance as a freelance contractor is also easy. One of the differences is you have a choice between types of membership plans. Free membership is available for all contractors, but you have the option of upgrading to a paid membership level. Fees vary depending on the plan you choose, ranging from free to a large business membership. I go into this in much more detail in Chapter 3.

Follow these steps to become a contractor:

1. Go to the homepage and click **Sign Up As a Contractor**.

2. Fill out the online form and create a user name and password.

3. Click the **Register** button at the bottom.

4. Choose the Elance category you want to work under, as shown in Figure 2.3. Categories are groups of contractors that provide related services. You can easily change this later or add more categories. You'll learn much more about this in Chapter 3.

5. Next, choose your individual or business membership level, as shown in Figures 2.4 and 2.5. These will vary in both cost and features, and in whether you want to register as an individual or a business contractor. I cover them in much more detail in Chapter 3. For now you can get started with the free one.

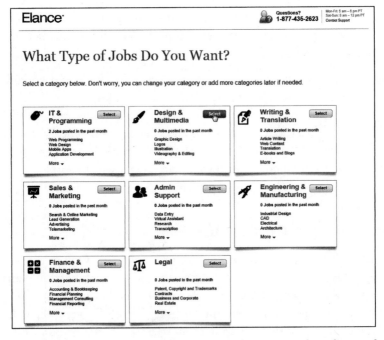

Figure 2.3: *Contractors are grouped into specific categories depending on the services they provide.*

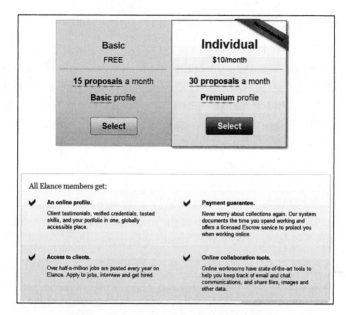

Figure 2.4: *Individual membership levels.*

Figure 2.5: *Business membership levels.*

Connects

Connects are a virtual form of currency used by contractors to submit proposals on open jobs. The number of Connects required per proposal varies according to the type of job posting and the budget of the job. Each Elance membership plan comes with a monthly allocation of Connects ranging from 15 per month for free memberships to 60 per month for a Large Business plan.

One of the most important reasons Elance uses the Connects system is to ensure that clients receive relevant proposals from contractors who take the time and effort to deliver a thoughtfully prepared proposal. By limiting the number of proposals that a contractor can make, this system acts to limit "spammy" proposals.

Spamming proposals is an unsavory and uncommon method of trying to win jobs. The contractor creates a generic proposal and copies and pastes it into as many project postings as possible in the hopes that something will stick. However, because Connects have a cost associated with them, this rarely happens anymore.

Depending on the type of Elance membership you enroll in, your unused Connects might roll over from one month to the next. You can also purchase more Connects, once again, depending on the membership plan you choose.

The Critical First Impression

Getting your account opened is easy and fast enough. However, now it's time to step back and consider who you want to present yourself or your company as. You must consider how you can showcase yourself in the best light to reflect your professional qualities. The idea is not to be someone you aren't, but to clearly reveal the best that you are.

When we're face to face with people, most of the messages we send are through nonverbal communication. Our words eventually lodge themselves in the minds of those around us, but not until these same people have already received and processed boatloads of impressions and formed opinions. There's no right and wrong about this, it's simply the way the human mind is wired.

The online world is much the same. What we actually type out matters, but so does how we present ourselves and the care we take in each detail. First impressions become so firmly ensconced in the mind that it can take an enormous effort to change them. In other words, first impressions stick.

TOP TIPS

Your information is safe online within the Elance system. Potential clients cannot see any information you don't want them to, like financial or personal details. Because of this, you can place extensive prior work experience data in your profile.

The key in the online world is to take this need for a positive first impression and turn it into an advantage. In this new way of doing business, you can study how you will present yourself as a client and freelancer. With Elance, you can slow the process and design your own first impression. Your unique personality will come across in your Elance presence.

Your New Work World

Several different opportunities exist for you to present your online image. The key is to remember that the little details add up. Let's go back to the person walking into the business meeting. If you're decked out in your suit and tie but haven't shined your shoes since the beginning of time, someone will notice. How about if the collar on your shirt is frayed or you're only wearing one cuff link? Sounds silly, but it all adds up.

The same goes with your online image. Pay attention. It's worth it for the freedom you gain. You can now be sprawled on the couch with curlers in your hair and a cat on your lap, while your online image reflects the sparkling professional you are in the virtual work world.

Why You?

For freelancers, this is the question that will cross every client's mind when they're considering which contractor to hire. And this is the question you must guide them into answering in your favor. An important part of the process will be covered in Chapter 6. But your image and therefore your sales presentation start with the first impression.

If you keep the question "Why you?" in your mind as you build your online persona, you will make better marketing decisions. It's the accumulation of details and the overall effect they have that will lead the prospective client to you like bees to honey.

Be the 10!

In the freelancing and small business worlds, online or otherwise, the 80–20 rule is alive and well. In fact, you could take it one step further and call it the 90–10 rule. Meaning, 90 percent of freelancers and small businesses do just okay, or outright fail, while 10 percent really shine. Ten percent of small businesses generate 90 percent of the revenue.

Don't let this dissuade you. By reading this book you're already well on your way to being in the 10 percent. You have the potential to glide right by the remaining 90 percent. Take these tools and strategies to heart. There is a reason the 10 percent succeed, and it has nothing to do with Harvard degrees or Daddy's rich friends. It's crafting your image, following through with what you say you'll do, and producing quality work on time.

But you must apply what you learn, and only you can do that.

Think Like a Client

If you're a contractor, this is the angle you must take to help give you the edge you need. If you're constantly asking what a client would think, you're placing your priorities appropriately. Being a successful freelancer isn't about talking about yourself, it's about discovering what the client really wants and then giving it to him.

CYBER SNAGS

One of the biggest mistakes contractors make at the beginning is not taking the time to truly understand what the client is after. They instead worry if they can convince the person to hire them. If you can write down the client's main goal in one or two sentences, you are well on the way to avoiding this pitfall.

If you're going on and on about what success you had at XYZ Corporation, the client's eyes will glaze over and they'll be on to the next contractor before you can say, "Look at me!" The way to gain someone's interest is to talk about them, not yourself.

Be a Client

If you really want to get inside the head of a client, there's a great way of going about it. Become one yourself. Find a project you need doing, post it (as explained step-by-step in Chapter 11), and you will be off and enjoying the wondrous experience of cloud collaboration.

For example, maybe you have a website that needs to be updated. Can you think of a new widget to add to it that you could contract out? How about getting research done to deepen the marketing angle of your business plan? Or what about the family's best pie recipes bound in a book for your mother-in-law's next Big 0 birthday? It can all be done on Elance.

Get started with a small project to experience the process and understand firsthand what your future clients will experience.

What's Sealing the Deal?

Survey results give us fascinating insight into what clients are actually looking for in an Elance contractor. Are the PhDs at the top? Is ageism preventing those over 60 years old from getting the best projects? Do you feel like if you could just move to the city you'd have more opportunities?

In fact, these were the bottom three criteria for who gets hired on Elance according to client surveys. The top criteria turned out to be what other clients said about previous work done, and work samples presented in the contractor profile (see Figure 2.6). In other words, it all boiled down to who could get the job done best.

What are the top criteria you consider when hiring online?					
	Most important	Important	Neither Important nor Unimportant	Less important	Least important
Feedback/Ratings	**64%**	33%	3%	<1%	0%
Work Samples/Portfolio	**63%**	36%	1%	0%	0%
Costs/Rate	**30%**	59%	9%	2%	<1%
Certifications and Skill Tests	**17%**	46%	25%	10%	3%
Location	**2%**	21%	32%	20%	25%
Degree from Well-known University or College	**1%**	6%	35%	29%	29%
Age	**0%**	3%	31%	23%	43%

Figure 2.6: *Survey results on hiring from Elance clients.*

Interestingly, although cost was rated important by 89 percent of respondents, it was rated most important by only 30 percent. The vast majority of clients wanted the job done well even if they had to pay over the lowest bid. Age, college degree, and location ended up at the bottom. Welcome to doing business in the twenty-first century.

Who Would You Hire?

None of this should come as a surprise, and as you gain experience with hiring on Elance you'll agree. The ability of contractors to post previous job feedback, as well as work samples and a work portfolio, gives clients much of the information they need to make informed decisions.

Worried because you're starting out on a new venture and don't have feedback or work samples to provide? Don't worry. I cover tips for beginning contractors in Chapter 8.

Red Flags

In much the same way that the online system lets quality contractors and clients come together, it also alerts you to those with a more passive approach to their online business. Red flags abound and with a bit of attention you can easily spot them.

Low *ratings* and negative *feedback*, little if any repeat business, and a poorly thought-out profile are the obvious issues. When a client searches through potential contractors, these statistics will stand out. Once again, the key is to make sure the impression you leave with your contractor or client is that of a professional at every level. Not everyone does, and this is good news for you.

> **DEFINITION**
>
> **Ratings** and **feedback** are both ways Elance clients convey the work experience they had with a contractor. Ratings are on a scale of 1 to 5, with 5 being the best. Feedback consists of written comments about the project.

The Competition

Hundreds of thousands of individuals and businesses have joined Elance, and there's no sign of slowing—the growth rate has been in the double digits since inception. The sagging global economy, corporate layoffs, and Teflon-strength entrepreneurial spirits will continue to fuel this growth. Given this business environment, it's more important than ever to understand your competition.

For clients seeking to expand their business through the use of online hires, growth means the opportunity to choose from an expanding pool of talented contractors. A client's competition is for the time and attention of the top contractors. This can be significant and sometimes solved only by larger and higher-paying projects, or by being a repeat customer. With the Elance system you cannot search amongst clients and see what they're up to and what you might learn from them. Your worldview is of contractors.

For contractors, however, the story is different. You might end up bidding on a job with dozens of other freelancers. It's important that you understand who your competition is and how to differentiate yourself. This is also a great way to get ideas as you build your own profile.

Remember, just because you have competition doesn't mean you can't come out on top. Online work sites are increasing in demand because people are finding work and are learning to build new lives; not because they're all crashing and burning. As the number of contractors grows, so does the number of projects posted.

One of the keys to being in the top tier is to understand who else is out there.

Research

Researching the competition is most crucial for contractors. As a freelancer, you need to understand who else is out there and what they're saying about themselves. So let's roll up our sleeves and start digging.

To get a general overview, log in to Elance and in the top-left corner hold your cursor over Hire. A drop-down menu will appear. Click on **Search Contractors,** as shown in Figure 2.7.

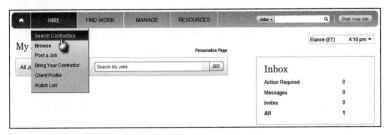

Figure 2.7: *Studying contractors will help you understand your competition.*

Next, on the left side of the page, click on the category you want to research and this will bring up a list of every single contractor registered in that field.

Several ways exist to narrow your search. Scroll down on the left side and you'll see you can sort by Tested Skills, Location, Feedback, Reviews, Hourly Rate, and Groups (see Figure 2.8). You can also access a list of somewhat different features by going to the Sort By drop-down menu in the top-right corner.

Figure 2.8: *Click on the contractor category to search for those contractors with similar specialties.*

Much information can be mined from learning what other contractors are doing. Spend some time here; you'll be grateful you did.

What's Working and What's Not

The idea is to generate ideas for your own business. You'll see many successful contractors as you explore Elance. Don't worry about them being your competition, you have something distinct and special to offer, and you can become as successful as you want to be. But learning from others is a proven strategy for giving yourself the extra edge.

TOP TIPS

Knowing what your competition is doing can give you some handy tools and ideas when it comes to designing your own Virtual You. Gather tips and dodge mistakes; it all boils down to research.

You can learn from those on the top end, and those on the bottom. Have a look at what the most successful are doing and also at those who aren't getting the business. Your eyes will be opened. Take notes, because in Chapter 4 we're going to put this all together and build your profile.

To Niche or Not to Niche

As you sift through the contractors, you'll notice some specialize very precisely, and others are available to do most anything within their category. This is a decision you need to make, too.

Volumes have been written on the advantages of providing a specific service with excellence, called niche marketing. This means becoming the "expert" in a narrow field and taking on the role of the go-to person. Yet others embrace the benefits of generalizing. With this approach your clients can get a variety of services from the same individual—you!

The answer goes back to who it is you want to be. Either method works; the key is deciding what fits best for your personality. Would you get bored doing the same work all the time? Or would you see the refining of quality as an ongoing challenge? Would you like to have a variety of projects, or would this lead to too much chaos in your organizing style?

You're the only person who can answer these questions. Be aware of the differences and get right on with designing your Virtual You.

The Least You Need to Know

- You can open your Elance account either as a client or contractor.
- Don't underestimate the importance of managing the impression you leave with others online.
- It's great practice for clients and contractors alike to get going with a small project.
- Research contractors and learn from the statistics and impressions they provide.
- Being a generalist or a niche marketer both work. You get to choose who you want to be.

Selling Your Services as an Elance Contractor

Although this part is devoted to contractors, Elance clients will be well served to read it as well. Understanding the freelancers' world is helpful in finding the best contractors to hire.

I review the different account types available and how Elance makes its money. But more importantly, the contractor will learn how to design a profile and online image that will help him or her attract the best clients. I share techniques and tips to win great projects from the competition, including how to write effective project proposals, but I don't stop there. Part of the process to becoming a successful contractor is won during the job itself. I discuss how to utilize the Elance platform to manage your jobs easily and effectively and how to develop a real connection with the client. This in turn will help bring in repeat business and referrals.

I end this part with an entire chapter devoted to the new Elance contractor. Every Elance member was once new, and I show you ways to help you get started quickly, and how to build your positive online reputation.

Contractor Accounts and Fees

In This Chapter

- The pros and cons of the basic account
- Individual account perks for $10 a month
- The hows and whys of business accounts
- How Elance makes its money
- Increasing your Connects and categories

When you're initially starting your freelancing business, every penny counts. The good news is that Elance individual and business accounts exist that are completely free of monthly charges. These have limited features, but you can easily get up and running. When the time is right, you can upgrade to a paying account.

At the same time, Elance is no charity. It's a for-profit business that provides a valuable service to freelancers and businesses alike. I explain the commissions charged on each transaction, and what kind of binding commitment clients and contractors make when they initiate jobs.

Lastly, what do you do when you're on a roll but are restricted by the number of proposals and/or categories in your monthly plan? It's all covered here, including one-off or regular monthly options automatically deducted from your Elance account, bank account, or credit card.

Account Types

First, let's look at what type of account will suit your situation best, including what type of fees you'll be paying. You can easily change between account types, add Connects, and even build a contractor team.

Four types of Elance accounts exist for contractors, as shown in Figure 3.1. They include both individual and business accounts, and also a basic option that has no monthly account fee.

Elance				
Edit Membership Plan				
	Basic	**Individual**	**Small Business**	**Large Business**
Marketplace				
Proposals to Clients • Monthly Quota	Up to 15	Up to 30	Up to 40	Up to 60
Profile Keywords • Appear in more search results	5	10	15	20
Hosted Portfolio	✓	✓	✓	✓
Add to Proposal Quota		✓	✓	✓
Add More Categories		✓	✓	✓
Preferred Placement in Search Results		✓	✓	✓
Workplace				
Users	1	1	5	unlimited
Storage	500 MB Per Work Room	1 GB Per Work Room	1 GB Per Work Room	2 GB Per Work Room
Guaranteed Payment • Automated Billing • Time and Milestone Tracking	✓	✓	✓	✓
Free Wire Transfers • One Free Wire Transfer per Month	✓	✓	✓	✓
Cost				
Monthly Membership • Cancel at any time	FREE	$10	$20	$40
Service Fee • Included in Proposals Presented to Clients	6.75% - 8.75%			
	○ Basic/Individual ○ Basic/Business	○ Individual	● Small Business	○ Large Business

Figure 3.1: *The Elance membership plan grid.*

The Basic Elance Account

This account is an easy way to get started if you're gradually working into a new freelancing venture. As you grow and gain experience, you'll want to upgrade to get added benefits including *preferred placements* in the search results and a greater number of monthly Connects.

A **preferred placement** is also known as a sponsored placement. This feature highlights your proposal and places it at the top of the client's proposal list. Although preferred placements give you extra visibility, be aware that they also cost you more Connects. Three preferred placements are allowed per project posting.

The advantage to the basic account is it's free of any monthly account charges. The disadvantages are you have a limited number of Connects and cannot add more. You also cannot add more categories to submit proposals in, and you do not have the preferred placement option.

Finally, in the basic account only a limited number of keywords are available for clients to search for your specific services. This can matter because a keyword is the intuitive word a client will use to search for contractors. Think of using Google or some other search engine. The words you type in to start your search are keywords. With Elance you have the opportunity to list keywords that will bring up your profile when clients type the same word(s) in the search box.

Individual Accounts

The next step up from a basic account, individual accounts give you a surprising amount of extra features for only $10 a month. The number of Connects you receive every month is doubled, from 15 to 30, as are the number of keywords clients can search by, from 5 to 10. You can add more Connects at any point if you run out, and you can sign up for more than one category. The preferred placement option is available for your proposals.

For single operators, this is a great option. If your business includes more than one person, however, you need to look into business accounts.

Business Accounts

Three options for business accounts exist: the basic account, which is free of a monthly account fee, and both small and large business accounts.

The drawbacks of the basic business account are the same as with the individual basic. You cannot add Connects, register in more than one category, or use preferred placements for your proposals.

The main attraction for a paying business account is that more than one person has access. As well, the number of Connects you receive each month is increased, as are keywords and storage space, and preferred placements are available. For a busy team, this is really the only viable option. The large business account has a whopping 60 Connects, 20 keywords, and 2 GB of space per workroom. Not bad for only $40 a month.

Elance Fees

Elance makes its money in three ways: account fees, service fees, and through the purchase of extra Connects and categories. Each of these is borne by the contractor as opposed to the client, and you should be aware of this as it will come into play when considering a price for your services (covered in Chapter 6).

Account Fees

As you can see from the membership plan grid shown previously in Figure 3.1, Elance account fees range from no charge to $40 per month. You can upgrade or downgrade at any point in time, and the fees can be taken from your Elance funds, bank account, credit or debit card, or PayPal.

Service Fees

Service fees are charged on each project payment and are taken out of the contractor side of the equation. The quote you give your prospective client in your proposal includes the service fee. Therefore, as you build your business and budget for expenses, remember that a commission will be taken. What you bid is not what you receive.

The standard Service Fee is 8.75 percent for those client relationships that generate less than $10,000. If you design a logo for a small business and charge $500, you'll receive a total of $456.25 in your Elance account at the end of the job.

CYBER SNAGS

It is against Elance rules to meet a client on Elance and then conduct work and get paid outside of the Elance payment system. You and the client are bound through Elance for 24 months, after which time you can work together away from the site. You agree to this within the Terms of Service in the account opening process. You can opt out of this agreement by paying a onetime $750 fee to Elance.

A discounted Service Fee exists and is 6.75 percent for those client relationships that exceed $10,000 in revenue. For the first $10,000 you generate from that client, you will pay an 8.75 percent commission on each payment received. It's only when you exceed that amount that the commission will drop to 6.75 percent for all transactions with that client above the $10,000 mark. Every penny counts, and this rewards long-term relationships.

Connects and Categories

Each proposal "costs" a certain number of Connects. The larger the job budget, the more Connects required to submit a proposal, and preferred placements cost more Connects, too (as you can see in Figure 3.2).

Included in your monthly membership plan is a set number of Connects that are replenished each month. Therefore, as the momentum in your freelancing business builds, you may need more Connects. When I first started with Elance, I had more than 20 proposals out at any one time. I certainly needed more Connects.

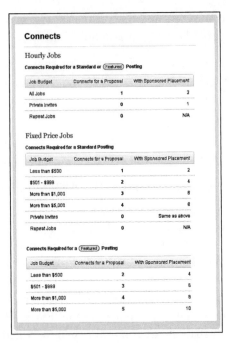

Figure 3.2: *Each proposal submitted costs a certain number of Connects.*

You may also find that you want to add more categories to your membership plan. One category is included, but you may want to add services from others. Paying membership plans allow you to add more. You cannot bid on projects that aren't in your category.

Purchasing both Connects and additional categories is easy. Just follow these steps:

1. Log in to your Elance account.

2. In the top-right corner will be your Elance user name. Click on this and a drop-down menu will appear, as shown in Figure 3.3.

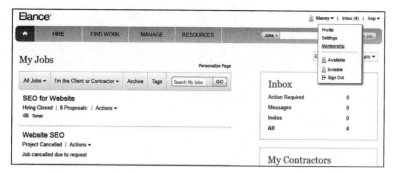

Figure 3.3: *From here you can manage your Elance account and membership.*

3. Click on **Membership**. From here you have two ways to purchase Connects. On the left side beneath the Membership heading, you can click on **Add Connects**. From this location (see Figure 3.4) you can purchase a onetime bunch of Connects, which will expire if unused at the end of the month. Or you can add this new number of Connects to your monthly plan. They will then be added and billed automatically each month and any unused Connects will roll over to the next month.

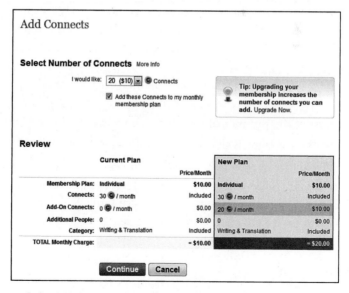

Figure 3.4: *Add Connects to your regular monthly payment, or purchase a set amount one time.*

You can also purchase Connects by clicking on **Edit Membership** on the right side of the membership page. From this location you can increase the number of categories as well, so let's go there for this example.

4. Click on **Edit Membership**.

5. Scroll down to Modify Your Proposal Quota. Directly beneath this is the Category box where you add or switch categories you can solicit jobs from, as shown in Figure 3.5.

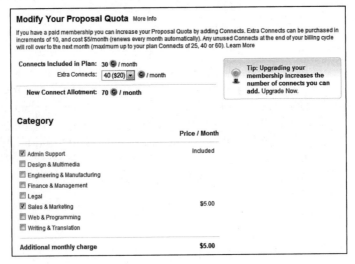

Figure 3.5: *Elance allows you to tailor your account through the purchase of additional Connects and categories.*

6. Select the number of Connects you wish to add and any additional categories. The costs are clearly displayed.

7. Scroll down to the Review section, as shown in Figure 3.6. This is where you can see the differences between your current plan, and the new one you have built. If you're happy with your new plan, click **Continue**.

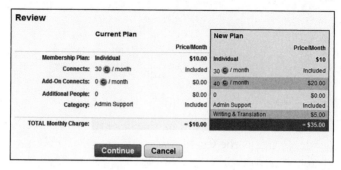

Figure 3.6: *View your changes before you confirm them.*

The Least You Need to Know

- There are limitations and benefits of the free Elance accounts.
- The quantity of Connects, categories, and keywords vary with each type of account.
- Elance charges contractors commissions on each transaction.
- You can purchase additional Connects and categories.

Contractor Profiles That Sell

In This Chapter

- The different profile views your clients will see
- Accessing and editing your profile
- The importance of the tagline, overview, and service description
- Keywords and their crucial role
- Your job history and statistics

Critical to being a successful contractor on Elance is creating a clear and concise profile. This is the go-to area where you parade your special talents and services, and you're able to demonstrate how you stand apart from the crowd.

Developing your profile isn't difficult; in fact, Elance makes it surprisingly easy, but it is a process where you must spend time and thought choosing how you will best present yourself. A sparkling profile sends one message, where a sloppy one sends another. If you're serious about building your freelancing business on Elance, the profile is your opportunity to strut your stuff.

In this chapter, I'll walk you through the process of building your winning profile, step by step. Let's get started!

The Elance Advantage

With a bit of time and thought, Elance gives you the advantage of being able to stand back and assess your image, make necessary adjustments at any point in time, and add a variety of bells and whistles so your professional image stands up and shines.

TOP TIPS

In the virtual work world, meeting face-to-face with clients is no longer common or even necessary. Because of this, you must take advantage of every online opportunity you have to present yourself in a positive light. This will help you stand out from the pack and become a top-dog freelancer.

As you present yourself in the online work world, you don't have to worry if your mascara is running or if your tie is crooked. You can now sit back, carefully consider how you appear online, and feel confident in the fact that you're putting your best image forward.

The ability to halt time and make sure you always look your best is an online advantage that offsets disadvantages, like not meeting face-to-face and developing that certain type of chemistry. In the years I've worked on Elance, I've met in person only one client. I've emailed, message boarded, Skyped, and talked on the phone, but almost never sat down at the same table.

In this rapidly growing new way of doing business, a person's presence has morphed from flesh and blood to pixels and hues. Run with this! Don't shy away and say it's not for you. Rather, realize the advantages—and there are many—and wallow in them. Elance provides the venue and tools to make it possible.

Profile Views

First, what am I talking about when I go on about this wonderful Elance tool called a profile?

The first shot clients will see of you is minimal but gives relevant data. They will find you either through a contractor search like I went through in Chapter 2, or via the proposal you submit. Either way, they will see something similar to Figure 4.1.

Figure 4.1: *This thumbnail view of your profile is chock-full of information.*

Basic information is presented such as your average rating, earnings over the past 12 months, and number of jobs. The first couple of lines of your overview are displayed, and the client can click on **Portfolio** and directly access your work samples.

TOP TIPS

Each view of your profile carries the message of your professionalism. Examine each one to make sure it's telling your story in the best possible way. This is a way, once again, to set yourself apart from the competition.

By clicking on the name of your business, a potential client is taken to your main profile page, such as the one shown in Figure 4.2.

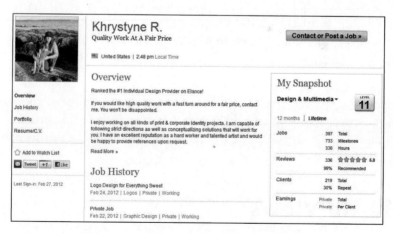

Figure 4.2: *The contractor's main profile page.*

Now we're getting to the good stuff. At a glance, prospective clients see a picture of you, get an overview of your business, have a snapshot of your work statistics, and can begin scrolling through your job history. On the left are links directly to relevant areas.

Let's go over each element of the profile in detail. But first, how do you get to where you can create and/or edit it in the first place?

Finding and Editing Your Profile

Navigating within Elance is easy, but as with any website, sometimes it takes a minute to see where you are and where you need to be. You can begin to create your profile in the account setup process or you can wait until later.

If you build your profile when you set up your account, you'll be automatically guided through the process. You won't need to search for where to go.

> **CYBER SNAGS**
>
> Don't write out your profile once, at the beginning of your Elance career, and then never revisit it. As your business grows, you'll have more services, samples, and freelancing sparks to keep your profile fresh and updated.

However, not only will you want to plan how you present yourself, you'll also want to go in and edit your profile periodically. As you gain more experience, get more marketing ideas, and build up portfolio samples, you can easily add these to your profile.

To access your profile away from the setup process and in the edit mode, simply click on the **Find Work** box at the top of the Elance page. A drop-down menu will appear. Click on **Contractor Profile**, as shown in Figure 4.3. This will take you directly to the profile edit screen (see Figure 4.4).

You can also click on your user name in the top-right corner of any page. A drop-down menu will appear; click on **Profile**.

Now you're ready to get in and get going. Just click on any of the blue edit buttons to bring up that section of the profile.

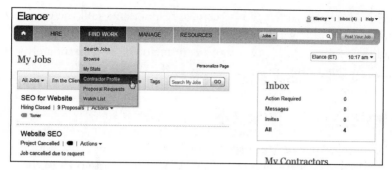

Figure 4.3: *Navigate to your profile from the Find Work drop-down menu.*

Figure 4.4: *Build and edit your profile.*

Painting the Profile Picture

Clients understand there's more to getting a job done than hiring the first contractor that pops up on their screen. They will research the proposal you submit, and then they will go to the business description you showcase in your profile. Your profile is part of you and your proposal. Don't underestimate its impact on your sales.

In a 2011 Elance survey, 65 percent of respondents said the online profile or resume was more effective in landing a job than a traditional resume. That's a significant majority, and fortunately, building that online presence is easy to do.

Upload a Photo

The more connected a prospective client feels to you, the more likely she will hire you. It's human nature. We prefer the known to the unknown. Obviously, there are limits as to how well your client is going to get to know you, but posting a photograph on your profile page is a surprisingly effective way to start breaking down the barriers.

Think of how you react when you see an actual photo versus that strange blue-gray generic silhouette. The photo brings you closer to the person. It gives that extra human touch, which is what so many people are looking for today. These details add up and make you a more desirable hire.

Make sure your photo is clear, tasteful, and shows you in a positive light. Swimsuit and party shots should be left for your Facebook postings. And if you have a business membership, you have the choice to use a logo instead of a personal photograph.

Profile Basics

Clicking on the first blue edit button will bring you to the Basic Information page. However, there's nothing basic about this. It carries some of the most significant information you'll be presenting. I'll start at the top.

Display Name

This is the name you'll be seen by on Elance. You have two options for how you want your display name to appear: your full first name and then your last name's initial, or your entire first and last name. The choice is yours.

Tagline

The tagline is simply a marketing phrase for your business. It doesn't have to be grammatically correct, and you have a lot of room to be serious—or play a bit.

Examples are:

- When Words Escape You, They Come To Us
- I.T. Outsourcing @ Peace of Mind
- We Deliver. You Prosper.
- Superior Ghostwriting, Editing & Proofreading

Minimum Hourly Rate

This feature is optional. Maybe you don't work on hourly projects, or you simply don't quite know how to price your services yet (see Chapter 6 for some guidance). But setting expectations is a great habit to get into. The services you provide have value and should be treated as such. By setting a minimum standard, you begin to communicate your financial line in the sand.

When you set your hourly rate, Elance will do the math for you so you clearly see what you will make after the standard Service Fee has been subtracted.

YouTube Video

Too high tech for what you had in mind? Don't let this intimidating thought prevent you from utilizing this great feature. Just like with uploading a photo, clients are more likely to hire someone with whom they feel like they have a connection.

A YouTube video is a great way to let the prospective client see you and/or your work setup. If you're a team, introduce the members. If you're flying solo, get creative and provide a snippet of your life as a freelancer, all the while aiming your presentation toward why you are the best person for the job.

Overview

The overview is one of the most important parts of the profile. The first couple of lines are visible in the contractor summaries seen when searching for contractors. And when the full profile is brought up, it's the first block of writing on the page.

TOP TIPS

A rule of thumb in writing is the first line, then the first paragraph, and finally the first page are the most important in any book, article, or essay. It is at these points that you are able to hook the reader. That is, gain their interest so they read more. Your overview is where you do just this.

At the top of the overview, your Minimum Hourly Rate automatically appears. Below this is where you get to capture the imagination of the prospective client.

Think about your profile from the point of view of the client. What does he or she want to know about you? How many pets you have? That you recently became a yoga instructor? That you, alone, sighted a UFO in the Arizona desert? Maybe … but more likely they want to know *why* you're the best person for their job.

As you consider what to say in your overview, have a look at what some of the most successful Elance freelancers have written.

The NetMen Corp, a wildly successful Elance graphic design business based in Buenos Aires, Argentina, starts with:

> "The NetMen Corp offers professional and high-quality logo and graphic design services at affordable prices. Our work is 100% original and 110% satisfaction guaranteed."

To the point, positive, and confident.

Khrystyne Robillard-Smith, Elance's top individual design contractor, says this:

> "If you would like high-quality work with a fast turn around for a fair price, contact me. You won't be disappointed. I enjoy working on all kinds of print & corporate identity

projects. I am capable of following strict directions as well as conceptualizing solutions that will work for you. I have an excellent reputation as a hard worker and talented artist and would be happy to provide references upon request."

Both these examples answer the question, "Why me?" They directly address the client's number one concern, who should she hire to get her job done?

In a strange twist, the overview is more about the client's needs than it is about you. The key is to show how you are the solution they need. It doesn't need to be long or fancy. Direct, positive, confident, and professional are the ticket.

As with all the elements of the profile, search through successful contractors and see how they've presented themselves. Don't copy what they say; clients can smell ingenuousness from a cyber-mile away (as well, it's just outright wrong to copy). But get a feel for how they show prospective clients that they're The One.

Service Description

This is where you go into more detail about the services you provide. You can really toot your horn here. It's your chance to explain what you do and what your background is in essay format. Where the overview is shorter and limited, the service description can include many details and facts that you want to be included.

TOP TIPS

Even though you have the ability to wax weary with your literary prose in the service description, try to keep your most relevant, positive, and/ or prestigious information near the top. As worthy as your writing may be, clients are busy people and may not read all the way to the bottom.

Start with a core business description like you did with the overview but add more details. You can also include personal details, provided they're relevant to your work on Elance. Avoid extraneous information like how big your family is or the Siamese fighting fish aquarium you recently purchased.

In the next few paragraphs you can then explain your background and who your team is, if relevant. Always keep in mind the contractor's mantra, "Why me?" Yes, the service description is about you. But it also explains to the prospective client why you're the best person for the job.

If you've had different jobs and career paths that might not be relevant to your current Elance goals, you can still include these. Just be sure to tie in why they'll make you a better contractor. Perhaps you have more life experiences, a more diverse range of talents, or wide-ranging interests. These can all help, but it's your job to lead the client into understanding why.

For example, raising 11 adopted children will most certainly make you an excellent time organizer. And having worked in the financial services field will have helped you understand the importance of client follow-up and satisfaction.

Payment Terms

This is yet another opportunity to set up project expectations right from the start. Here you outline how you prefer to get paid. Do you expect a deposit up front? Do you require milestones? Or is waiting until the end of the job and your client is 100 percent satisfied until you get paid one of your contractor-added values?

You can make this section as long or as short as you like. And go into detail or simply hit the basics. The choices are yours. The information will appear on the Resume/C.V. page for individuals, and on the About the Company page for contractor businesses.

Keywords

Keywords are what prospective clients use to find contractors for their jobs. A client could type in "ghostwriter," "virtual assistant," "logo design," "JQuery and JAVA Script," or any other service they're looking for.

At the top of the Search Contractors page is the box where they enter keywords or the name of the contractor, shown in Figure 4.5.

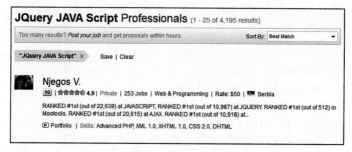

Figure 4.5: *Clients use keywords to search for contractors with specific skills and services.*

The number of keywords you can be identified by depends on the type of membership plan you have. Remember, keywords are a crucial way for clients to find you and check out your services. Carefully think through which ones will be of most value. If you were looking for your services, what words would you search with?

This takes you to the bottom of the Basic Information section of the profile editing page. Click **Save** and you will be taken back to the main editing page.

Job History and Snapshot

At this point you've completed the Overview section of your profile. This is an extremely important area for you to spread the message of your talents. But we're not done yet.

The job history and snapshot areas of your profile highlight the work you've already done on Elance, as shown in Figure 4.6. Obviously at the beginning you won't have any numbers here (see Chapter 8 to learn how to get started quickly). But as you progress and build your Elance career, these numbers will reflect what clients can expect from you in the future. Hence, they're incredibly important.

Figure 4.6: *Your job history and feedback give important information to prospective clients.*

Clients will go to your statistics not only to see how active you are on Elance—a sign that you're serious about your business and deliver quality goods—but also to check out the feedback left by other clients.

> **TOP TIPS**
>
> One way to get great feedback is to simply ask for it. I always set up the expectation right at the beginning that I was working for positive feedback. Then at the end, I asked for it again. If you follow through on what you promised the client, there's no reason for her to not give you a stellar rating and feedback.

Good feedback is crucial and something you need to proactively work on. I show how you can do this in Chapter 6. You also have a chance to respond to feedback. This allows you either to compliment the client in return, or to explain why something went wrong if the feedback is less than expected.

Levels

You will see a *level* designation on the Job History page. In Figure 4.6, the contractor's level is 10. The level is a way Elance ranks you according to a proprietary algorithm. In a nutshell, it's calculated, among other things, on the quantity of work you've done, the ratings and recommendations received, your job acceptance rate, the number of tested skills you take, and the quantity of verified credentials you have.

> **DEFINITION**
>
> A contractor's **level** refers to their activity and achievements on Elance. The higher the level, the greater that individual's or business's activity, earnings, and positive feedback.

For an individual contractor, the levels range from 1 to 12—the higher, the better. For companies, they range from 1 to 17. The way to make sure your level is as high as possible is to work toward the preceding criteria. Elance Terms of Service violations and jobs cancelled due to poor performance would be negative factors in the calculations.

Your Portfolio and Sample Work

This is your time to shine. By posting sample work you've done for Elance clients or otherwise, you let prospective clients see just how spectacular you are. If you're a designer, post the best projects you've designed over your career. Do you build websites? Display them here. The same goes for samples of your writing, architectural designs, or whatever else you can use to showcase your talent.

The portfolio can be seen in a gallery view, with snippets from each project, as in Figure 4.7. Or the viewer can click on the actual image for a close-up of the work (see Figure 4.8).

Figure 4.7: *Displaying work samples lets clients see and understand the services you provide.*

Figure 4.8: *Showcasing your talent helps you win jobs.*

Don't underestimate the opportunity to display your work. It's here you can prove just how good you are. If you don't have any samples yet, don't worry. As you grow you will accumulate them, so just come back and post them in your profile then.

Skills

The Skills section allows you to rate your work skills using an Elance test. The results are compared against every other person who took the test at Elance, as shown in Figure 4.9. If you score well, this is a great way to stand out. Conveniently, if you don't score well, you can choose to not display the results. You can even retake the test down the road when you've honed your skills a bit more.

The system also allows you to self-rank yourself in the skills areas. Many contractors do this, but it really doesn't prove anything. I mean, are you really going to rank yourself low in a skill and then post it? But the option is there, nonetheless.

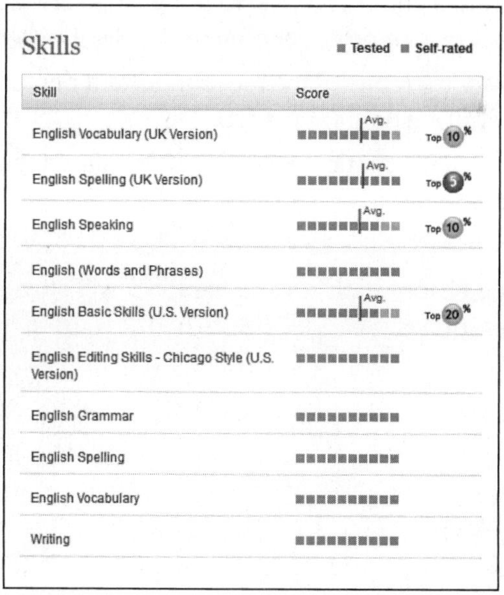

Figure 4.9: *Tested skills rank you against other Elance contractors; self-rating skills allow you to post your own score.*

Surveys have shown that clients do find it important that contractors take these tests. They like to see how potential hires rank in specific categories that will be of relevance to their projects. Also, taking skill tests helps raise your Elance level.

Employment and Education

The final areas for your profile are the most resume-like: your employment history and your education. As with any resume, online or not, take your time to highlight your best and most relevant accomplishments. Don't lie; it'll come back to bite you. Just showcase yourself in a positive light.

The Least You Need to Know

- Your profile is a vital window into the services you provide as a freelancer.
- Uploading a photo and/or a YouTube video are great ways to personalize your profile and bring the client closer.
- The overview is one of the most important descriptive pieces of why *you* are right for the job.
- The service description allows you to explain in depth what you have to offer.
- Keywords rock—use them effectively.
- Your job history statistics and feedback will blossom as your business grows.

Winning Projects as a Contractor

In This Chapter

- Finding projects to bid on
- Getting to know the potential client
- Good signs and red flags
- Key habits for your competitive edge
- The power of the personal connection

Many online jobs exist and more are posted each day, yet the contractors' virtual work world remains a competitive one. In an average month, more than 50,000 new jobs are posted on Elance, and almost double from a year earlier. At the same time, more freelancers are discovering the benefits of working online. Even large corporations are beginning to hire contractors to do one-off or full-time projects.

As commuting in the cloud becomes more widely accepted, you will be competing with more and more talented people across the globe. Fortunately, tools and techniques exist to help you do just this. Building a successful freelancing business isn't a matter of blindly submitting proposals and hoping the right client comes along and hires you. You can proactively target the best jobs, work your way up within the competition, and end up winning one quality job after another.

It is possible. But you must think smart and streamline your efforts. Ready to get started? Read on!

The Job Search

Part of the process of targeting clients you've done already. In Chapters 2 and 4, you learned to step back and take some time in designing the virtual you. By clearly showcasing who you are and what services you provide, you are targeting clients. This is the first step.

The second step is covered in this chapter and begins with choosing who you want to work for. Don't just sit back and hope you land a good client. You will win more projects when the services you provide match up directly with what the client is asking. Roll up your sleeves and do what you can to make it happen.

For a start, let's look at what jobs are being posted, and then consider who's posting them.

Finding Jobs in Your Category

To find jobs on Elance do the following:

1. Click on **Find Work** in the main top toolbar.

2. In the drop-down menu, click on **Search Jobs**. This will bring up a general chronological search of all jobs posted on Elance.

3. To narrow your search, on the left-side menu, click on the category you're registered under. Within this, click on any subcategories you're interested in, as shown in Figure 5.1.

If you don't click on any subcategory, all jobs within your main category will be displayed. But for any subcategories you click on, jobs will be filtered to include those only. You can go as broad or as narrow as you like.

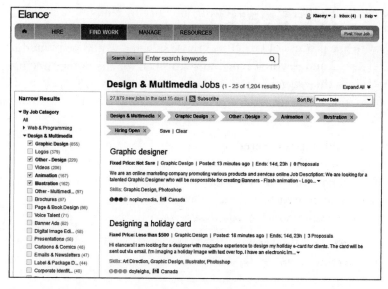

Figure 5.1: *You can bring up all jobs within your category, or filter for those within select subcategories.*

TOP TIPS

It's fine to narrow your job search as far as possible into subcategories. But be sure to also cruise through the main general postings. First, you may be surprised by appealing work in other subcategories. Second, the client may not have clicked your favored subcategory when he posted his project description.

But don't stop here. You still have several more ways to filter your potential jobs.

Price and Time

If you keep scrolling down the menu on the left you'll find filters for price and time, as shown in Figure 5.2. Again, these help you tailor the selection of jobs you have to choose from. These filters are not perfect. Like with categories and subcategories, great jobs can slip through the parameters.

I scored a long-term article editing job once by applying for a job I'd found under a much lower price range than I was targeting. But the posting said it was a trial and those selected would be invited to longer-term positions. If I had only searched for the higher paying jobs, I wouldn't have found this. Be flexible!

Figure 5.2: *Rather than scrolling through all jobs available in your category, filter for those segments that appeal to you.*

Using these menu items, you have a wide range of choices. You can choose between hourly and fixed-price jobs, and you can set the price range for each. By clicking **Go**, the system immediately applies these new parameters.

The advantage to selecting only Featured jobs is that these cost the client an extra $25 to $35. The implied filter here is these clients are more serious because they paid extra. Payment Verified means the client has had her payment method verified by Elance. It's a good thing.

Next, you can choose those projects that have just been posted, those posted within 24 hours, or those that are nearly expiring. Many contractors believe the first proposals in have an advantage. Others believe they get the edge by being the last one in. The theory there is if the client had found who he was looking for, he would have awarded the project already.

CYBER SNAGS

Don't get caught in the trap of rushing your proposals so you're one of the first ones bidding. The quality of the proposal is far more important than the speed with which it arrived. If you submit hurried, inferior proposals it will only hurt your prospects for winning the job.

The key is you have choices. Use them. Experiment. See what works best for you.

That Little Box in the Corner

Finally, you have one more job search method within this page. In the upper-right corner of the Job Search page sits a little box preceded by the words "Sort By." Click here to bring up the drop-down menu shown in Figure 5.3.

Figure 5.3: *From this one drop-down menu, you have many ways to filter job postings.*

Consider these additional filters as you refine your search. Some overlap, yet some are unique like high and low budgets, and proposal counts.

Saving Searches

When you've narrowed your searches to make sure you're getting the right type of jobs, you can actually save these parameters and have a new search emailed to you every day or week. This is a handy tool to save time.

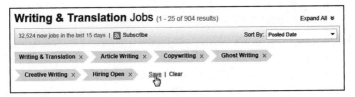

Figure 5.4: *Saving your search parameters is easy, and Elance will email you new search results every day or week.*

To save your search parameters, simply click on the **Save** button, as seen in Figure 5.4. Elance will then ask you if you want them emailed daily or weekly.

Maximizing Client Searches

An often-overlooked key to getting the best jobs via invitation is understanding how the Elance system works when clients search for contractors. Think of it as looking at the other side of the coin. Just like a contractor searches for jobs using certain parameters, clients search for contractors using parameters.

You can take valuable steps to make sure you get maximum exposure through the Elance search engine. The search engine will look for the following data:

- **Keywords.** Choose the ones a client would use to search for the type of job you want to do.

- **Skills.** Clients will select skill tests in their search criteria. Go through the available Elance skill tests and choose 10 of them that fit the work you do. Self-rank at the beginning if you must, and then take the actual tests later. When a client searches for contractors with these skills, you have a higher chance of being seen.

- **Hourly rate.** Choose an hourly rate because, once again, this is a criteria clients search with.

- **Verified credentials.** The search engine emphasizes contractors with verified credentials. This designation helps you get a higher Elance level ranking.

By maximizing your criteria for client searches, you stand a better chance of getting higher up in the search results and therefore noticed. Every little bit helps.

Assessing Jobs

Now that you know how to search for jobs, it's time to have a deeper look and assess which you want to bid on. Remember, it's not just the job that's important, but the client, too. You want to take on the kind of work you love, but also do it for someone who will treat you right.

In the following sections I'll give you two examples. One is of a client that potentially looks very positive. The other is one with some red flags to keep in mind.

Lookin' Good

Within each job search result, you will get the gist of the project. In Figure 5.5, the job title explains what this client wants in a nutshell, when it was posted, and how many proposals have been received so far. If you hover your cursor over the proposal count, a box will appear with the current bid range.

Figure 5.5: *The basic job and client data.*

At the bottom of the snapshot, you can see where the client is from but also other valuable information. Place your cursor over the client's user name and a box comes up with valuable statistics.

> **TOP TIPS**
>
> As you search through job listings, use the Add to Watch List feature to keep a short list of jobs you're interested in bidding on. This will give you a chance to sift through this refined group later and choose the very best to begin with. You can also streamline the workflow because first you're finding jobs, and second you're bidding on them.

In the case of Figure 5.6, you see the total the client has paid out is over $5,000. The award rate for jobs is 100 percent—26 out of 26 jobs have been awarded. Many times clients will post jobs and then never hire anyone. You are told where the client is from, how long they've been a member of Elance, and whether or not their payment method has been verified by Elance.

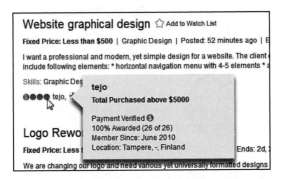

Figure 5.6: *Client statistics at a glance.*

The little green circles denote the award rate at a glance, and if the first one has the dollar sign in it, payment has been verified. Overall, this client looks great. He or she is serious and experienced with Elance. If the job itself is of interest to you, click on the **Add to Watch List** button.

The Project Description

Click on the name of the project and this will bring you to the Project Description page. Here, again, you have a plethora of information to work with (see Figure 5.7). I'll use the same project as before.

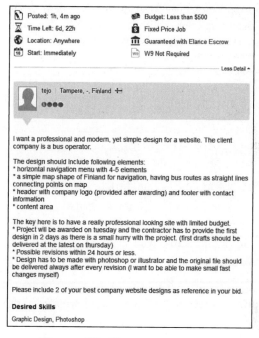

Figure 5.7: *The project description.*

At the top of the project description is basic information about the time and price parameters. The project posting itself is the meat of the business. The project is reasonably clear given the simple nature of the job. A website needs to be built and these are the conditions.

The Client Profile

Any time you click on the client's blue user name, you will be brought to the client's profile and feedback area. See Figure 5.8 for an example. Here you will see much the same statistics that you saw earlier. However, crucial to your client research is the feedback area.

Private Job

My Rating for this Job		Contractor: Private
★★★★★ 5.0		Jun 9, 2011 | Private | Graphic Design | Completed | Job Details ⌄
■■■■	Quality	
■■■■■	Expertise	**Feedback Comments:**
■■■■■	Cost	"Great & creative provider! Worked hard to exceed my expectations. Will use, and am actually
■■■■■	Schedule	already using again!"
■■■■■	Response	—Client
■■■■	Professional	

Private Job

My Rating for this Job		Contractor: Private
★★★★★ 5.0		Jun 3, 2011 | Private | Graphic Design | Completed | Job Details ⌄
■■■■	Quality	
■■■■■	Expertise	**Feedback Comments:**
■■■■■	Cost	"Great provider and very responsive to customer needs!"
■■■■■	Schedule	—Client
■■■■■	Response	
■■■■■	Professional	**Contractor Feedback Comments for Client:**
		"Teemu is one of the client that you really will be happy to work with, detailed project, knows what they want and timely feedbacks. Looking forward to collaborate with Teemu again. God Bless!"
		—Contractor

Figure 5.8: *Client feedback on other contractors' jobs is important to review.*

Scroll down the list of jobs the client has awarded. This shows the feedback and comments the client gave. It also gives you an idea of how busy they are. Notice how this client appears to be enthusiastic and positive. He or she is involved in great working relationships. This is a good sign.

Beware of a client that consistently leaves negative feedback. They may be difficult to work for or have unrealistically high expectations.

TOP TIPS

If you're a new contractor, positive clients can be jewels. They give great feedback for a job well done and ask for repeat business—just the things you need to get a good start. Make sure that in your proposal you let the client know just that: You're a new contractor and want to work hard for them to earn great feedback and repeat business. They'll appreciate your honesty and enthusiasm.

As well, notice how in one of the comments the client left, remarks are made about repeat business. This is interesting indeed, and exactly what you're looking for. If I were bidding for this job I would make sure to nurture this relationship very well.

Red Flags a Flyin'

There is no guarantee that every time you think you've found a great client, she'll actually turn out that way. Or if you think you're dealing with a dodgy one, you end up right. But paying attention to clues is prudent and, over the long term, will pay off.

Figure 5.9: *Client data often reveals potential red flags.*

In Figure 5.9, we see some client statistics that should cause you to pause. None of this is definitive, but you might not put this job posting in your A list. Let's look at why.

Right off the bat two things stick out: the fact that they only have a 35 percent award ratio and the low total dollar amount given that they've awarded 26 jobs. A low award ratio can simply mean the person is busy. But here, a lot of jobs have been posted, 74 in all. Why would they go to the trouble to post so many and then not award them?

Next, the average price paid for each job awarded is $79. This is far too low. If your guts are telling you this client is looking for cheap work, you might just listen. But let's look further (see Figure 5.10).

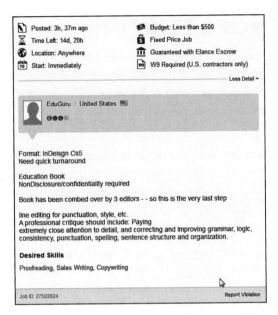

Posted: 3h, 37m ago
Time Left: 14d, 20h
Location: Anywhere
Start: Immediately

Budget: Less than $500
Fixed Price Job
Guaranteed with Elance Escrow
W9 Required (U.S. contractors only)

Less Detail ▲

EduGuru | United States ▥

Format: InDeisgn Cs5
Need quick turnaround

Education Book
NonDisclosure/confidentiality required

Book has been combed over by 3 editors - - so this is the very last step

line editing for punctuation, style, etc.
A professional critique should include: Paying
extremely close attention to detail, and correcting and improving grammar, logic,
consistency, punctuation, spelling, sentence structure and organization.

Desired Skills

Proofreading, Sales Writing, Copywriting

Job ID: 27502624   Report Violation

Figure 5.10: *This project posting has some red flags.*

First, remember from the project title in Figure 5.9 that the book they want copyedited and proofread is 500 pages long. That's no small project. And from earlier we already know that they usually pay low.

TOP TIPS

As you gain experience with bidding on and completing projects, you will begin to develop a sixth sense as to the quality behind the posting. Pay attention to this, and if in doubt, ask the client questions in your proposal to clarify issues.

Next, they claim the book has been reviewed by three editors already and just needs a final review. However, if you read the description closely, they're also saying it needs a review for logic, consistency, sentence structure, and organization. Five hundred pages' worth? I would run, not walk, away from this project. However, if you really want to give it a try, ask to see a sample of the work.

Utilizing the New You

I'll get into the nuances and structure of crafting your project proposals in Chapter 6. What I want to discuss in the remainder of this chapter is how to use the new you so you stand out in the bidding process.

Part of winning jobs is writing great proposals, but another equally important part is how you behave as bidding is open and the client is considering who to hire. Here, too, you can stand out and I'll show you how.

First, you must understand the client to the best of your ability. By researching their history with other contractors on Elance, and as you learn what type of feedback and comments they give, you begin to understand what they value. This homework provides excellent information.

Which Projects to Bid On

Ideally, you should choose those projects you're most qualified for and can prove this through your portfolio, feedback, work experience, and/or references. However, also choose those that get your heart pounding. If you're enthusiastic about the job, your client will feel this through your communications. Enthusiasm is contagious and everyone wants to feel like their project is exceptional and exciting.

If you don't have the expertise or credentials built up to bid on the best projects, bid on those that are similar but smaller in scope. Or bid on those that cover one aspect of the larger, more attractive projects. This way you can build up feedback and references from clients in related areas.

Part of the reason you're building your freelance career is for the ability to do more of what you love. Don't forget this and get sucked into the same-ole same-ole jobs you might have had in a previous incarnation. Get your pulse racing and clients will respond.

Developing a Competitive Edge

In order to stand out from the crowd, you need to develop good habits in the bidding process. This is that time after you've submitted your proposal, and before the client has chosen her contractor. Fortunately, this isn't difficult. Many top contractors use these same good habits to develop their competitive edge.

TOP TIPS

The keyword to win projects by is *quality*. In the end, this is what the best clients want. Quality includes doing a great job in an efficient and positive way. The better you can communicate this, the more jobs you will win.

There's a bit of an art to honing your bidding skills. Over time you will develop your personal style that works for you. Allow for this. Don't try to fit into someone else's mold. Learn from the best, apply what works, and add everything else you've found that works for you. Here are a few habits used by top contractors in the bidding process you might consider:

- Give prompt responses to questions or requests for more information from the client. This is part of your job. Show them you're available and professional.

- Ask intelligent questions. This will show you've carefully considered their unique situation and have found an area that needs clarifying.

- Don't deeply under- or overbid. I'll get into pricing in the next chapter. But for many clients, under- or overbidding is an immediate put-off.

- Provide samples, especially if they request them, but don't overdo it. One hundred and fifty of your best websites will exhaust the client before he even begins reviewing them. Pick those that most resemble his project, and say you can provide more on request or to view the Portfolio area of your profile.

- Bid on new job postings. This is a point that some contractors debate. However, see if it works for you as it does for many. Search for the most recent postings and bid on those to start with.

- If you have a significant language barrier with the person you're submitting a proposal to, have someone check your writing. Hire an Elancer to do it on a regular basis. Poor grammar can be tolerated to a certain extent, but after a certain point it becomes a burden.

- Craft your proposal following the guidelines in the next chapter.

These habits aren't foolproof, nothing is, but they will help you stand out as a quality contractor eager to work.

Making the Personal Connection

The personal connection is what it all boils down to. By the follow-up and follow-through outlined previously, you are able to make a connection with your future client. Your client will see you through the rest, and recognize the quality you bring.

But you must work the process. Don't simply submit a gazillion proposals and wait for good fortune to fall into your lap. Unfortunately, it doesn't work that way. Good fortune responds to a targeted, streamlined process done repetitively. By reading this chapter and applying what you've learned, you'll be well on your way to standing above the rest.

The Least You Need to Know

- Use the categories and other filters on Elance to narrow your project search.
- Project descriptions are often very revealing. Pay attention to positive signals and red flags to know what each is really telling you.

- Save your search parameters and have them automatically emailed to you every day to streamline the search process.
- Assess client statistics and feedback to see if this is someone you want to work for.
- Every single interaction you have with a client before you are awarded the job is part of your virtual "interview." Be enthusiastic and professional.
- Develop positive, proactive habits to stand out from the competition.

Crafting Killer Proposals

In This Chapter

- Making the personal connection with your proposal
- A beginning proposal structure
- Learning from a sample proposal
- Pricing your services
- An alternative proposal technique

For a contractor, the proposal is one of the most critical tools you have available to win jobs. Here you have the opportunity to make your first connection with the prospective client and to explain why you are the best person for the job. Unfortunately, this is also where most jobs are lost.

As much as you have time and space to sell yourself, if you don't turn this opportunity into an advantage it can work equally hard against you. More jobs are lost through sloppy, ill-prepared proposals than anywhere else. This is good news for those of you reading this chapter.

I will provide you with key points to consider, a general structure to follow, and a sample proposal to work from. (In Appendix B you'll see more sample proposals.) I'll also go over pricing strategies, and the unique approach to proposals by one successful contractor that will get your brain spinning. Read on!

First Contact

In Chapter 2, I emphasized the importance of first impressions, and how this applies just as much online as anywhere else. Oftentimes your proposal is your first contact with the client. If they've hunted you down and invited you, perhaps not. But 9 times out of 10, the beginning of your Elance journey will be the first they've heard of you.

If the majority of jobs are lost here, then you have the opportunity to really stand out. The key is to not be sloppy or flippant, but to apply practical solutions and attention to the project.

TOP TIPS

Remember the three-legged stool of winning projects: craft a killer proposal; build a portfolio that showcases your talents and answers the question, "Why you?"; and be prompt and professional in your follow-up and replies to client queries. By doing these three things well, you set yourself up for success.

In the next sections, I provide you with the tools to do just this, but I want you to remember and emphasize the fact that herein lies a big part of your road to success. Pay attention to this crucial first contact and have fun with it. Your attitude will come through loud and clear. Let's begin.

Let Them Know You Listened

This is single-handedly the most critical element of the proposal process. The client doesn't really care about all the wondrous accomplishments the contractor throws at you—they want to know if you can do their job and do it well. That's it. Once the client understands this, then they're more interested in what else you've done.

First and foremost you must make sure the client knows you listened to them in their job posting, that you understand what they need, and that you can do it for them. Three key things. If you don't understand exactly what they need, that's fine. Ask. This also shows you are listening and definitely works in your favor.

When you have shown the client these three things, you will stand above the rest. If your price is higher than your competitors', then you will be able to justify it. I'll get into pricing later in the chapter. First let's look at the key elements of the proposal.

It's About the Client

It's amazing how many times this little nugget flies right by contractors who otherwise have the best of intentions. The proposal isn't about you and what wondrous things you've accomplished. It's about the client. Focus on this one element and you'll be pleased with the results.

Explain to the client what they will get when they work with you. How will they win by awarding you the job? This will answer the question, "Why you?" which is lurking in the back of their minds. You'll have time to tell them about yourself as well, but that's not the primary purpose of the proposal.

Be Genuine

This goes back to the chemistry and personal relationship that you hope to build in the bidding process. A lack of genuineness can be smelled a mile away, and it's not a pleasant aroma. Clients aren't stupid. If you're plastering on a fake cyber-smile and kissing their virtual backsides, they're going to know it.

CYBER SNAGS

Saying "I've read your proposal, understand what you need, and would like to work for you," sounds all well and good, but it doesn't prove anything. You could cut and paste that onto any job posting. Prospective clients sense this. Create an opening that is unique to that one client.

Instead, try to find a connection. Bid on projects that inspire you and this will come through naturally. If they have a website, visit it and let them know you did. If they want you to edit a manuscript, comment on the content itself. Hopefully it will be interesting to you and you can let them know. If you have a personal connection with the subject matter, this is an excellent advantage.

Genuineness is a crucial step in creating the personal connection that will win you jobs and create long-term relationships. You can't build a home on a crumbling foundation, nor can you build a relationship on insincerity. If you're not feeling the mojo and can't get excited about the project, then maybe it's not for you.

Plan of Action

By now the client knows you're thinking of her, and that you're a genuine person living deep within her monitor. Next is to establish a clear plan of action for completing her project. Lay out when you can begin, what steps will be involved, and your estimated completion date.

Highlight the stages the project will require. If different versions, mockups, or drafts are needed, state when you will have them done for review.

The plan of action is the meat of the issue and it needs to be clear and concise. Bullet points are fine, or something more casual, whatever your style. But now you're appealing to the practical, get-it-done side of the client. Imagine it's like the sound of heels clicking on the marble floor of a long, empty hallway. Tick off the various steps involved.

Questions and Ideas

Asking questions and presenting ideas and solutions to the client that he might not have thought of are excellent ways to build rapport. By asking a question, you show you're involved and thinking about the job. You will also gain valuable information about the details of the project.

Sometimes the only way you can really understand the vision the client has is by discussing it with him. He may want a website with X, Y, and Z features, but what does he really see when he thinks about it? By asking intelligent, well-placed questions, you can find the answer.

Don't go overboard with this. One or two questions are fine, five or six are not. The same goes with sharing ideas. You want to show you're already thinking of the project, not that you want to completely redesign it. If appropriate, share one idea for improving the concept and explain why it should work. Make sure they understand it's optional, and that you're just thinking of how to make their widget that much better.

In the current form of the Elance website, you can't ask a question via *workroom messaging* until after you've placed your initial proposal and the client has initiated communication first. Therefore, you must get your questions and ideas into your first proposal.

> **DEFINITION**
>
> **Workroom messaging** refers to the Elance system that allows clients and contractors to communicate via a message board in each project workroom. All communication here is stored and saved so you can easily refer to it later.

Another option is to add them later and resubmit the proposal. This accomplishes two things. One, you get to ask your questions and share your ideas. Two, you get in front of the client twice and hopefully in a positive way. This will make your name more familiar.

Why Me?

Although you know the proposal is about the client and his needs, and you'll be faithfully expressing that you understand how to do the job superbly, you must add a dollop of why you are the best choice. The key is to keep this short and zeroed in on the project itself.

> **TOP TIPS**
>
> Find the core goal of the project—Droomla website, ghostwritten autobiography, logo design for a medical group—and link your expertise directly to that goal. This is how you can show the client you are the best person for the job.

If the client wants a flash website, state you're an expert in flash websites, having done X number of them in the past year (assuming you are an expert in them). If they need a technical manual edited, state your specific experience and how it relates to the project at hand. Having won an award for your screenplay may look great on a resume, but it has no relevance to the technical manual and that client's editing needs.

Enthusiasm Is Contagious

If you're hyped up about the client's project, they will sense this and respond positively. But, as I mentioned previously, it must be genuine. This is why one of the keys to success is to bid on projects that you are truly excited about.

The client cares about her project and wants it done well. Why else would she be on Elance? If you care, too, and are enthusiastic about it, this will increase the personal connection exponentially. It's really the best thing for both sides. Why become a freelancer if you don't love your work?

The Copy and Paste Folly

Don't do it. Don't even think about doing it. If the personal connection is what will get you the job, then copy and paste is the opposite and what will lose you the job. I know it's easier, I've done it. I know it's faster and you can get more proposals out this way. But so what?

Taking the time and paying attention to the client's needs will get you more jobs and better ones. This, after all, is the goal. In the long run, copy and paste will waste your time and lead to frustrating rejection after rejection. Don't do it.

Basic Proposal Structure

Each proposal will be different, as is the personality of the individual writing it. There is no perfect one-size-fits-all proposal template, but you can work from a basic structure. Over time and as you gain experience, you will morph this into your own style.

Consider the following structure:

- Introduction paragraph clearly stating the client's primary project goal and your expertise in solving it.

- Mention you've included one to three samples of work that are similar to what they're looking for.

- Your plan of action.

- The timeline for completing the project.

- Questions and/or ideas.

- Why you? A short paragraph touting both your enthusiasm for the project and any other accolades you feel are relevant and important. Mention high feedback ratings on Elance.

- End with a polite sign off and offer to answer questions or provide references (if you have them).

Given all these elements that need to be included in your proposal, you may think it'll end up being several pages long. In fact, the elements work together to create proposals that are short and concise but pack a punch.

This structure will serve you well as you begin your freelancing career. Include these key elements specifically tailored to the client in a friendly, upbeat way. You will quickly get the feel for it and make your own adjustments.

Sample Proposal

What follows is a sample proposal to give you an idea of what the end result will look like. Notice that it's not long, but was obviously written with the specific client in mind. It's succinct, enthusiastic, and confident. I've included comments in bold.

Dear George,

I specialize in unique and creative webpage designs. Your veterinary project involves an extra layer of creativity and writing which is the part of design I love. I have included links to two webpage designs with similar functions to yours. This should give you an idea of my conceptual thinking and humor.

A great start, stating the client's goal and that this is exactly what the contractor specializes in and enjoys. Links to samples of similar work are included. The key here is similar to the client's project, not just any website pages.

What I'll provide:

— 5 unique concepts for the homepage design consistent with your current look and brand.

— 3 redesigns based on feedback and discussion

— 1 design with a static display and unique elements

— 1 additional design using dynamic features to enhance the information

— Editable source files upon completion.

Concise plan of action and deliverables.

Timeline:

— First mockups of the 5 homepage designs by noon EST, Friday, Jan. 6, 2012.

— Redesigns and the static and dynamic designs by noon EST, Wednesday, Jan. 11, 2012.

— Final design assembled and delivered by noon EST, Friday, Jan. 13, 2012.

Fixed and reasonable timetable. You can ask if they need it sooner, but don't let the client rush you and risk producing inferior work.

What, specifically, do you want done with the newsletter sign-up form? I suggest a basic InDesign template, incorporating your brand and look. The center will use editable text and is where the info will be delivered.

Question and possible solution.

I am excited by this project and ready to get started. It lies exactly within my area of expertise and on previous jobs of this type. I have 100 percent positive feedback and recommendations. Please review my profile for the comments. I'm hard working and ready to make your project one more success!

The "why me?" paragraph. It's enthusiastic and mentions others have been pleased with her work, too.

Let me know if you have any questions or need any additional information. I can provide references on request.

Thank you for your time, Susan

The proposal ends politely with an offer of additional information and references.

That's it. It's not too scary or daunting, just thoughtful and tailored for the client. It also doesn't reek of salesmanship, which can be off putting to both sides. Sure, you must sell yourself, but there are many ways to do this.

Pricing Your Services

This is a sticky issue and has as many answers as there are freelancers. The fact is you must place a monetary value on your services that the market will bear. The good news is, as you gain experience and good feedback, the market will bear higher and higher fees—to a point.

In the Beginning

As you begin your freelancing journey and before you've built up self-advertising in the form of high ratings and feedback, you will have less power over your pricing. It's a fact. It's not beautiful, but it is temporary. This doesn't mean you need to be taken advantage of and work for peanuts. It means you'll make more money as you gain experience.

Initially, you need to base your pricing on what you see other contractors bidding, as shown in Figure 6.1. Study this. Look at similar projects and see what the bidding range is. Check out the price range on the projects you're bidding on. If you don't have extensive outside experience and credentials in your area of expertise, you will need to place your bid in the lower half of the range.

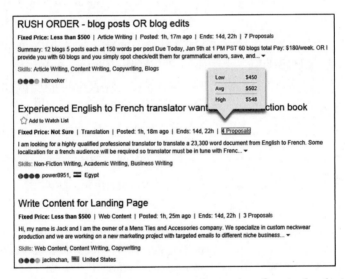

Figure 6.1: *By hovering your mouse over the number of proposals submitted, you can see the current price range of bids.*

TOP TIPS

If you're a new contractor but have extensive credentials and expertise in your field, you can choose to place your bids higher. Your job is now to make sure the prospective client understands your expertise.

Don't work for pay that's just too minimal. Sometimes the lowest bids are ridiculously low. Don't compete with these, ever. These lowball bids can skewer the price range and you might have to allow for this. Place your bid in the lower half or third of *realistic* bids. And if that's still too low, search for another job to bid on.

Remember, you're only doing this until you get your own feedback established. This might take you three or four jobs. Tell the client you're working hard to get your feedback established. It's the truth and most of them will love helping you out.

As You Progress

As that precious feedback builds up, you can sit back and reassess your pricing strategy. After all, the idea is to have a comfortable life to go with your work freedom, and for your talent and services to be valued.

At this stage ask yourself after each project, "Was it worth my time?" Working on Elance will help you establish your value to future clients. You will have proven you can do the work well and on time. As this continues, clients will pay more for you because you are no longer an unknown factor.

TOP TIPS

When a job is awarded to someone other than you, take this as a learning opportunity for pricing. Assess the winning contractor's profile and experience, and what their amount was compared to yours. Do this regularly and you will be keyed into what your competitors are charging.

Eventually you will set your own price ranges. It's a gradual process but one that works. You will find where you fit within the market. If you begin to bid too much, you will lose out on the better jobs. You'll notice this and bring your prices back in line.

A Pricing Formula

Once you have good feedback and therefore the ability to set your own prices, how do you know what they should be? Several factors come into play and they will vary depending on your specialties.

For hourly jobs you must arrive at a fee that's competitive yet pays you appropriately. Study your Elance competitors but also the industry standards for your services. Over time your experience and feedback will justify higher fees, especially if you specialize. Clients understand value and are willing to pay for quality. You will have a feel by now for what your competitors are charging, and you can adjust your rate accordingly.

For fixed-fee projects, pricing is a little more complicated. Many times contractors still boil it down to what they will be making hourly. This is because the main product contractors provide is brain power, or put another way, time. In this light, consider the following formula:

- List all the project tasks that will need to be completed.

- Estimate the amount of time for each task.

- Include any expenses you'll incur, including Elance fees, office supplies, and even travel expenses if they apply.

- Tally all the hours and multiply by the hourly rate you would like to make.

- Add in your estimated expenses.

The issue then becomes, some projects run smoothly while others turn into nightmares. To allow for this you can create two scenarios based on the preceding formula. This is an optional step and if you've worked with the client before, it may not be applicable.

The first scenario would be the amount of time the project would take if it ran smoothly. The second would be if you ended up with the client and/or project from hell. What would this time-based result look like?

CYBER SNAGS

Most clients are fair and reasonable and want to get their job completed in the best way possible. Others, however, will test you and try to wring out every last nickel. Take this as a sign that they'll be difficult to work with in other ways, too. Carefully consider whether or not you really want to work with them.

Realistically, not all projects are made the same. If you come up with a normal and a "stressed" rate, you will have a range of prices to work within. Your final decision will be based on your impression of and history with the client.

Pricing Red Flags

Consider the following red flags in anticipating whether or not the project will run smoothly:

- The client is difficult to reach and slow to answer your questions.
- The client swears she will give you more work if you just do this one job cheaply.
- The project changes a lot during the bidding phase.
- The client is unsure about what the final result should look like but she'll "know it when she sees it."
- The client is indecisive when you ask questions.
- The client pressures you to lower your bid because everyone else is lower.

You will discover more warnings as you gain experience. When you see these, carefully consider if you really want the project, and what premium you will add price-wise if you do decide to bid on it anyway.

Negotiating

The vast majority of the time, stick to your price and don't negotiate. If a client tries to negotiate you down, how much are they valuing the services you provide? They're implying you overcharged them in the first place.

If you are willing to negotiate, know your bottom line in advance. State clearly to the client how much work is involved. If you really want the job and feel the client is being fair and honest, you can lower your price, but certainly don't make this a habit. Ideally, you will ask them to sacrifice something, too, like three revisions rather than five, or whatever would work in your specific case.

The Mechanics of Submitting a Proposal

It couldn't be easier. When you find a job that interests you (see Chapter 5 for steps to target the best jobs and clients), click on the title. This will take you to the Job Description page, which is also where you submit your proposal.

Figure 6.2 shows where you submit your proposal. You can also add attachments and choose to include or hide your contact info. Next, include your proposal amount and any milestones, as you can see in Figure 6.3. You'll see that the system automatically calculates the amount you will get paid after Elance's commission has been taken.

You can also wait and fill out the milestones for when you've been awarded the project. If the client awards the job to you, you will be notified by email and given the opportunity to fill out the terms and milestones. You must both agree on these before the project officially begins.

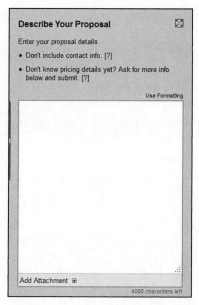

Figure 6.2: *Submit your proposal on the Job Description page.*

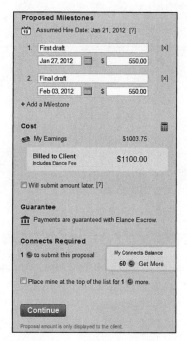

Figure 6.3: *Enter your fee and milestone details here.*

On the left side of your proposal page you can see who else is bidding (see Figure 6.4). You will not be able to see what their proposal says or how much they're charging, but you know who else is competing for the job.

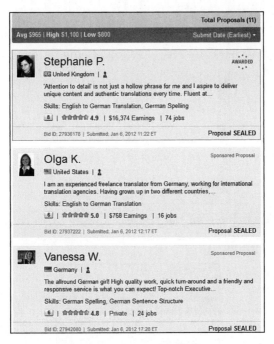

Figure 6.4: *The Job Description and proposal submitting page also show you who else is bidding.*

Next, you wait. If you want to get the client's attention or add any additional information or questions, you resubmit an updated proposal (which doesn't cost any Connects).

The Nonproposal Proposal

My goal in this book is to help you become as successful as possible with Elance. However, everyone is different. I can't know you and know what your individual personality and circumstances entail. So I must provide you with as much information as possible, and then you decide what works best for you.

In this light, I'd like to pass on the bidding technique of an über-successful freelancer named Alexander Rolek (his Elance user name is ARolek, and his website is www.tinyfactory.com). Alex designs mobile web applications and began his Elance career too broke to pay the $8 for a web domain name. (Now, let's face it. That's pretty broke.)

However, by using the bidding technique he shared with me, within 10 months Alex went from penniless to running his own company, Tiny Factory, in a 2,500-square-foot office in San Diego (not exactly the cheapest office space going 'round). He has become so successful he's fully booked with projects through the next quarter and literally has more work than he can do.

TOP TIPS

Combined with Alex's unusual bidding technique, he also carefully studied the market and his specific skill sets. He ended up focusing on a specialty that allowed him to become the expert in this area and charge higher rates.

Alex credits this all to Elance and the fact he never wrote a single proposal. I can hear you now, "What? Wait a minute, Karen. You've just spent the entire chapter telling me how crucial proposals are!"

Yes, I have. But have a look at what Alex does and see how his method accomplishes the same thing—establishing a personal connection with the client—but just in a different way.

Instead of writing proposals for each project he bid on, Alex asked questions. He felt that there was no connection with the normal proposal process, and he wanted to dig deeper into what the client wanted. Through this question-asking process, he developed a dialogue with each prospective client and therefore a personal connection.

He didn't even submit a bid amount until he knew the client better. To submit a proposal without a bid amount, click on the **Will Submit Amount Later** box in the Cost & Timing section of the proposal details as in Figure 6.5.

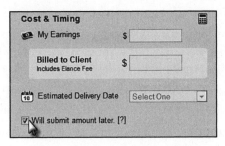

Figure 6.5: *Click the **Will Submit Amount Later** box to submit a proposal without a bid price. This allows you to ask questions before you decide on a fee.*

The client ends up spending enough time educating Alex on what he really wants that it's a waste of time to educate some other contractor. A comfort level is established between Alex and the client. Once Alex understands the project at a deeper level, he almost always goes for the highest bid. He estimates his success rate at 70 percent.

The questions Alex asks are designed to challenge the client; to get him thinking more deeply about his project. This back-and-forth communication stretches out the timeline between when the project is posted and when it's eventually awarded, but most of the time Alex wins the job. Because his award ratio is so high, he also uses fewer Connects—an added perk.

Because of his success on Elance, most of Alex's work now comes via referrals and job invites. And when you're invited to bid on a project, it doesn't cost you any Connects. Extra bonus!

Alex's logic led him to develop a relationship with the client before the project was awarded, and to understand what was needed so he could deliver it well and at a good price. He could only please the client if he knew exactly what he wanted. Makes sense, doesn't it?

This is one more method for you to mull over and see if it fits your personality and specialty. Give it a try and see if it works for you.

The Least You Need to Know

- The proposal is one of the most important tools you have to win jobs.
- The first key aspect of the proposal is letting the client know you understand their needs and can deliver on them.
- Use a proposal structure to make sure you hit each element and in the right order.
- Price your services by analyzing the time and costs involved, in relation to your desired hourly rate.

Managing Projects—Your Time to Shine

In This Chapter

- Organizing your job and communications through the workroom
- Using milestones and status reports to keep the project on track
- Building and managing your team
- Techniques to build your relationship with the client
- Setting work boundaries early

You've targeted the best jobs, beaten out the competition, and won the coveted projects. Now what? They say be careful what you wish for because you just might get it! Relax. This is the point when the fun begins. Your freelancing business is no longer a dream—it's a reality and that means it's time to act.

In this chapter, I'll show you the ins and outs of the Elance online work environment. The virtual workroom has all sorts of tools and features to help you conduct business smoothly. You can keep track of all your correspondence, monitor hourly projects and get paid on time, set milestones and request escrow funding and release, and easily share files and documents. And that's just the beginning.

As you work with the client, you will learn that this is a time bursting with opportunities to generate repeat business and referrals. Not only is the quality of the end result important, but also how easy and flexible you were to work with along the way. These are crucial aspects to bringing in more business and getting great feedback.

You've Been Awarded the Job, Yikes!

You will be notified by email and also on the Elance system itself when you are awarded a job. The email subject line will say congratulations and state the name of the project. The body of the email will contain a link directly to the project terms and milestones. When you click on this link, you will be able to accept the project and adjust any milestones necessary.

It's rewarding to be chosen for a project, especially if in the process you had to wade through a bit of competition. Congratulate yourself, go out to dinner or order in pizza as a treat. Then roll up your sleeves and get down to the business of managing your project.

TOP TIPS

Marketing your freelance business is an ongoing process. Every single time you communicate with your client you have the opportunity to be professional, competent, and positive. This will directly pay off in feedback, referrals, and repeat business.

First off, keep in mind that you will be constantly judged by the client. Again, it's how the brain works. Instinctively we assess people's actions and reactions and file them in the "I like it!" or "Wow, what's up with that?" folders.

Therefore, you need to always be thinking of this aspect of your online image. You can't smile and wave hello as you pass their office door, or offer them a Starbucks next time it's your turn to buy and deliver. But you can do the online equivalent. Don't overdo this, just pay attention.

The first thing you need to do when you are awarded the job is contact them through the workroom message board and say thank you. The power of those two words can move mountains. You can even let them know how excited you are to get going. It's true, and this is great PR. It takes you all of a few seconds. How cool is that?

Elance Tools

Elance makes it easy to conduct business online. This is no small feat. Think about it; millions of dollars are passed through the system as hundreds of thousands of projects of all types are accepted and completed. Most of these occur without a technical hitch.

Various tools and features exist that allow this work environment to function smoothly. I'll go through each of them.

The My Jobs Page

When you log in to your Elance account, you will automatically be taken to the My Jobs page. Here, all of your active jobs will be listed, as well as those that have been completed but are not yet archived.

You will refer to this page often so have a good look around. Consider it a key component to your virtual office. When you want to take action of some sort, you can come here to do it. To navigate back to the My Jobs page, simply click on the little house in the upper-left corner of the main Elance toolbar.

Figure 7.1 shows a sample My Jobs page. Notice how jobs are listed on the left half of the page in chronological order, with the most recently awarded projects at the top.

By clicking on the arrow on the right side of the project box, you bring up the milestones and billing summary for that specific project. At a glance you can see what's next and if you've been paid.

In the job box itself is an Actions button that when clicked on creates a drop-down menu with a considerable amount of choices. Clicking on any of the menu items will take you directly to the necessary page. This is a fast and convenient way to take care of business.

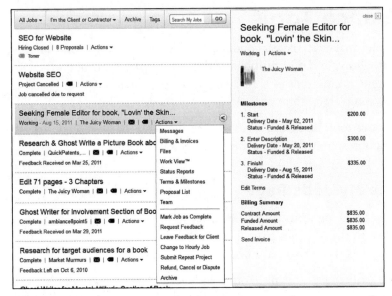

Figure 7.1: *The My Jobs page lists all your projects and is a go-to area for taking action.*

Workroom

If you click on the job title, you will be taken to the workroom for that project (see Figure 7.2). Here everything you see will have to do with that job and none of the others. The amount of information and features available are awesome. Take some time to explore where the various links and boxes take you. I'll point out the most used and important.

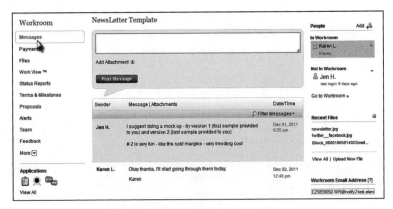

Figure 7.2: *The project workroom.*

The workroom opens up with the messaging board in the center. This is handy, as it's where much of the day-to-day activity goes on. The messaging system is set up so you receive them all via email as well.

An advantage to using workroom messaging is that all messages are kept within the Elance system. If you should have a misunderstanding or disagreement of some sort, you can always go back and see exactly what was said.

> **TOP TIPS**
>
> Clients may suggest using private email addresses to communicate, and this is allowed by Elance. However, remember to save all the emails in a specific file dedicated to that project. Also, only messages through the workroom are allowed in any Elance dispute process. Private emails are not.

On the left hand side is a menu of work areas you can access. Just click on the phrase and you will be taken to that part of your "office." For example, if you click on **Billing and Invoices**, you will be taken to the page that shows the record of all financial activity for that project and what's pending. In Chapter 15, I discuss in detail the financial aspects of working on Elance.

File Sharing

Sharing files and documents couldn't be easier. Simply click on **Files** on the menu on the left, and the file sharing page will pop up. Here you can see all the files stored on Elance, as well as when they were uploaded and by whom.

If you want to upload a new file, click on **Browse** and locate the file you want. Click on **Open**, then click on **Upload File**. It will appear in the shared file page.

Like with email correspondence, using the Elance system to store and share files is wise. It automatically creates a record of what's been done, when, and by whom. This is a great way to avoid misunderstandings. Everything's here, right out in the open, meaning you're well on your way to reducing work-related stress by avoiding it in the first place.

Terms and Milestones

This area helps enormously in managing your projects for meeting
expectations and deadlines. Milestones are used to schedule steps
along the way to project completion. Most often, each step also
corresponds to the contractor being paid a percentage of the entire
project amount.

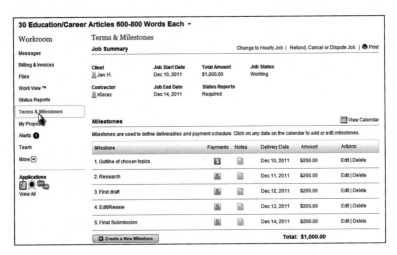

Figure 7.3: *The milestone feature is a great way to show your project's progress*
and get paid on time.

Each milestone description is outlined, as well as the delivery date
and the amount of payment, as you can see in Figure 7.3. The
milestones can be edited and deleted, and new ones may be added.
It's a fluid yet changeable system designed to provide structure.

CYBER SNAGS

A common mistake new contractors make is not clearly setting out
what steps are involved in delivering the completed project. Using the
milestone feature helps in planning the project, and in communicating
this plan to the client.

The Terms & Milestones page also allows you to upload project
agreements (which I cover in Chapter 14). At the bottom is a history
of all communication regarding changes. It's necessary for each party
to agree to any change before it takes effect. This, too, is documented.

Status Reports

Weekly status reports (see Figure 7.4) are required for each fixed-price project. The contractor submits an online report before midnight on Sunday. Elance will send you an email reminder a couple of days before.

30 Education/Career Articles 600-800 Words Each					
Workroom					
Messages	**Week Ending Dec 12, 2011**				
Billing & Invoices					
Files	**Job Status**				
Work View ™	● OK				
Status Reports	Milestone	Delivery Date	Percent Complete	Amount	Payments
Terms & Milestones	1. Outline of chosen topics	Dec 10, 2011	100% ▪▪▪▪▪▪▪▪▪▪	$200.00	Invoiced—Dec 10, 2011
My Proposal	2. Research	Dec 11, 2011	100% ▪▪▪▪▪▪▪▪▪▪	$200.00	Invoiced—Dec 11, 2011
Alerts	3. First draft	Dec 12, 2011	100% ▪▪▪▪▪▪▪▪▪▪	$200.00	Invoiced—Dec 12, 2011
Team	4. Edit/Review	Dec 13, 2011	80% ▪▪▪▪▪▪▪▪▪▪	$200.00	
More ▾	5. Final Submission	Dec 14, 2011	0% ▪▪▪▪▪▪▪▪▪▪	$200.00	

Figure 7.4: *Weekly status reports allow both you and the client to determine if the project is on track and if payments are on schedule.*

The status report is easy enough to fill out. It will include the date and a snapshot of the milestones reached and those left to go.

You have three options for designating the status of the project for that week: OK, Problem, or Complete. Click **OK** and green means go, the project is on track. If you click the **Problem** button, you will be asked to explain what the issue is. Complete means you've finished. Normally you only use this after the client has reviewed and approved the final material.

Whichever status option you choose, the client will be notified on the other end of that week's status report. You can also make comments on the project and upload attachments.

Keep It on Elance

Although not required, it's prudent to keep all communication within the Elance system. Obviously, this won't be possible with phone calls and face-to-face meetings, if you have them. But where possible, it's sound business practice to keep records of what's written and agreed upon. This is no different from traditional work environments.

We can design technology to be as flawless as possible, and yet glitches will still appear. The same goes for the human condition. As much as we like to think we're civilized and all grown up, misunderstandings occur, personalities clash, and expectations can be unclear or even imagined.

By keeping good records, you pave the way for reducing problems and solving them quickly should they appear. After all, just like in life, most are due to misunderstandings of what's expected. If you can whip out the email where you agreed to fluorescent green for those garden gnomes, rather than the puce the client thinks she ordered, you're set to nip the conflict in the bud.

Managing Your Team

If your freelancing business involves having a team, a few additional factors should be considered. The more people that get added to the mix, the better the job might get done, but also, the potential for loose ends or faulty seams increases. This isn't a bad thing, it's just something you need to be aware of.

TOP TIPS

The best freelancers abhor being micromanaged. Their entrepreneurial spirits demand the freedom to do the job in the best way possible, but as they see fit. If you're the team leader, use this to your advantage. Clearly explain what needs to be done, then get out of the way.

Teams are easily coordinated within Elance. Team members can be added in small and large business accounts. Small business accounts allow up to five team members, and large business accounts have space for an unlimited number.

Each team has slots for four roles:

- **Owner.** The team owner has access to all functions within the account, including the transfer and withdrawal of funds.

- **Administrator.** The administrator has much the same access as the owner, and can be assigned the administrative tasks of the project.

- **Account Manager.** This person has the ability to submit the proposals, send messages, file status reports, request invoices and escrow funding, etc.

- **Staff.** This person will be assigned a role and will work within his or her own workroom. Staff has no access to terms and financial information, and cannot withdraw or transfer funds.

Each project should have a team leader. That is, someone who coordinates who does what by when, and that each job is done in the best way possible. It's up to each team owner to determine who this person will be for each project. The progress of each member can be monitored by the leader, and any setbacks rectified without the client knowing anything was amiss.

Ideally, only one person will be in direct communication with the client. This may vary depending on the type of project, but as a rule of thumb, it's sound business practice. One person can better coordinate the flow of information and therefore avoid confusion and mixed messages.

The leader will also be responsible for making sure the milestones are met, and that any changes are clearly communicated up and down the line.

If your role is that of staff, your "boss" is the team leader rather than the client. Simple enough. Make sure you clearly understand what your role is—and if you don't, ask—and then hunker down and do it. Issues should be brought up with the team leader, not directly with the client, unless you've been given the okay to do so.

The Competitive Edge

Becoming a successful freelancer isn't only about scoring a few projects and delivering them on time. Growing a small business can be romantic in concept, but it can be all-consuming in practice. In order to preserve your sanity and make this early growing stage as painless as possible, things exist that you can do to let your clients do part of the work for you.

TOP TIPS

To succeed as a freelancer in the online world, each client project, interaction, milestone, and even dispute should be seen as a chance to exude professionalism and reliability. This is how you will stand above the rest, all the while sitting in the comfort of your own home, abiding by your own schedule and dress code.

A happy client is not only one of your best advocates, but also one of your most productive business growing tools. The goodwill that comes from them can lead your dreams into territory you never imagined. But you must nurture these positive relationships, and in return, they will come back to you in wonderful ways again and again.

Stay In Touch

If the most common cause of misunderstandings is faulty expectations, then it serves to reason that the solution is to excel at communication. There is no overestimating this one aspect of dealing with clients, online or otherwise.

As I have explained, critical to proposal writing success is clearly expressing that you understand what the client wants and can deliver on it. (Refer to Chapter 6.) But good communication doesn't begin and end there.

TOP TIPS

Some successful contractors make sure to communicate with their clients every single day. Depending on the project, this is a great way to let them know you've got their best interests in mind and are working hard for them.

As the project progresses, give your client updates, don't just wait for the status reports to be due. Ask questions if you have them, and let them know you're out there working. If you go silent on a client, she may wonder if you're actually doing anything and lose confidence.

Always let the client know if you expect any delay or significant change in the project plan. Clients are human; they understand that life happens to us all. If you get sick, have a family crisis, or simply underestimated the extent of the job, speak up. Let them know your situation and provide a revised schedule or set of milestones.

On the flipside, when your client contacts you, reply quickly. Think about how you feel when you ask a question of someone and they get back to you immediately. You feel valued and respected. This is exactly how you want your client to feel, too.

Take the High Road

As much as it hurts, as much as we want to tell 'em what we really think, it's better business to never respond in a harsh or combative way to a client. It's common sense. Always be polite, always let them know you heard them and will find a solution to whatever upset they may be having. Battling with a client is a losing proposition.

One of the advantages of working online is that you have time to take a walk, vacuum the ceiling, or hit whiffle balls off the deck until you cool down and think of the best and most logical reply.

Get Ongoing Feedback

Feedback at the end is great, but it's not going to ensure you're doing the best job possible along the way. It depends a bit on the project; some shorter ones may need no feedback at all. But it's a wise move indeed to stop and ask how you're doing.

CYBER SNAGS

Some freelancers make the mistake of disappearing from view once they get awarded the project. In their mind, they're working hard and getting the job done. But the client doesn't know this. Again, think like a client. Let them know what you're doing, ask for feedback, and stay in regular contact.

Some projects, like designing a logo or website, will require feedback. It's how the final design is chosen. But others may be more straight-forward. Whatever your project, try to give your client a taste of what you're doing and ask them if they like it. Two advantages come from this: you learn whether you're heading down the right road, and you have another opportunity to communicate with the client. It's a win-win.

The Extra Mile

Within limits, it's a good idea when possible to do a little bit more than you're asked to do. This sets the precedent of goodwill, which can then be returned in myriad ways.

As well, if it turns out that the project needs a little extra work done, something that wouldn't take a lot of time, consider including this at no cost. It doesn't lower your value, but instead shows that you're human and a good person to work with. Those are both qualities that will get you return business and referrals. Obviously, do this in moderation.

Boundaries

Given all the extra things you can do for your clients and ways you can show how professional and wonderful you are, it's also crucial to set boundaries. You do have value, and your time and talents need to be respected. When you set professional boundaries, your clients will respect you all the more for them.

What do I mean by this? At the same time that you want to be available for your clients and provide stellar service, you also need to look after yourself. Sometimes projects can turn into chaos if the client isn't taught that you prefer certain parameters around your work environment.

I had a client once that emailed me several times a day with extra stray bits of information for a biography I was writing. Another preferred long phone calls several times a week. This ate into my time and I wasn't getting paid anything extra for it. As a new freelancer, I also let my clients know I was available all weekend long. Good for business, bad for life.

Each person's boundaries will be different. You're freelancers, after all. The key is to step back and consider what yours are. What work environment do you want to create? If you lay it out tastefully at the beginning, this will preserve your sanity down the road.

Consider the following issues:

- Are you available on weekends?

- How do you like to be communicated with? By email/Skype/message/chat/text/phone?

- How often do you want to be given extra questions or information? At any time? Once per day/every other day/once a week?

- Do you have set hours you're available within? Like between the hours of 8 A.M. and 5 P.M. EST?

Maybe you're open for anything, maybe you're not. The key is to plan your world.

The Least You Need to Know

- The process of completing the job is full of opportunities to make positive impressions on the client.
- The My Jobs page and project workrooms are go-to areas for managing your business.
- Milestones allow you and the client to keep track of progress and get you paid on time.
- Teams can be set up with different member roles and individual workrooms for staff.
- Ongoing communication is crucial in creating client advocates.
- Set your work boundaries early and in a friendly, positive way.

Tips for Beginning Contractors

In This Chapter

- Getting your first project
- Quality versus price
- Learning to leverage your unique experiences and talents
- Common pitfalls to avoid
- The problem with underbidding
- Getting positive feedback

One of the questions I get asked most often about Elance is, "How do new freelancers get started?" If you don't have any ratings and feedback, what does the prospective client have to go on? Some new contractors are joining the Elance community because they've been laid off or downsized. Others want to supplement the family income with a side job. And some have a dream or passion they want to pursue.

All of these are not only viable reasons to become a contractor, but have been the motivations behind other successful freelancers. Everyone was new once on Elance. No one came here with ratings and feedback ready to go. Whatever your situation, if you work smart and learn, you can make it work in the virtual work world.

In this chapter, I'll cover tips and strategies from those who've succeeded, myself included. I'll build you a path through the cloud jungle, which if you follow will put you one great big step ahead of those who haven't read this book.

You Can Succeed

The freelance life is not for everyone. As romantic as it sounds to be tapping away on your laptop while sitting on the beach, umbrella laden drink at your side, reality is actually a bit different. It's true that as you succeed your lifestyle will become your own. If 3 A.M. is your optimal work hour, you can flick on the light and get to work while dressed in your PJs, the dog snoring at your feet.

But there's also the day-to-dayness of finding more clients, pleasing the ones you have, and—most important for some—not having the luxury of a steady paycheck. In short, freelancing isn't for everyone. But if it's for you, you can succeed if you're self-motivated and disciplined.

> **CYBER SNAGS**
>
> At the beginning, you may very well receive 19 rejections for every job awarded. This can be hard on the ego and lead you to wonder if you should bag this freelancing idea. Instead, the way to think of it is, you got one! Not that you lost 19. Perseverance pays.

So remember this as you move forward with your freelancing career. It's not always easy, and sometimes you'll think you're working harder than if you just had that regular paying job. But if you stick with it, the freelancing lifestyle can be downright amazing.

All You Need Is a Toehold

As with so many things in life, it's that first yes that matters so much. The first time you go on a date, the bank gives you credit, or investors help you fund your own business—it's getting the first yes that takes so much effort.

Once you get this toehold, you can leverage it to make the next yes's that much easier. In the case of freelancing with Elance, you must focus intensely on getting the first job. It may take you dozens of proposals submitted, or it may take just one. But focus on this until you succeed, then nurture that project like it's the newborn babe it is. From this point, you develop your reputation.

One technique some new contractors have used is to bring clients over to Elance themselves. Let's say you have a connection with a local printing shop to help design logos. Get the owner to post one of her projects on Elance. It's no cost to her other than the few minutes it takes to sign up.

Explain what you're doing and that this will help you grow your logo/design business. If you have a positive relationship to begin with, there's no reason why she wouldn't want to help out. As well, you may be doing that printing business owner a big favor by exposing her to the possibilities within Elance.

Quality Is Key

You may be thinking that the best way to get those first jobs is to underbid the daylights out of everyone else. After all, clients will surely go for the cheapest price, right? Wrong. Time after time, top clients say the most important consideration for them is quality.

Quality is your key. You must emphasize why you are the best person for the job, not that you're the cheapest. In fact, many clients automatically discount low bidders because they can't fathom how they can get quality work done for prices that are too cheap. And often they're right.

CYBER SNAGS

Equally important to not bidding too low as a new contractor, is not bidding too high. At this critical stage, you don't have the pricing power you will have later. At the beginning, place your bids in the bottom half to bottom third of the bidding range.

One of the single most important ways you can let a client know you've got what they're looking for is to make sure they know you've listened to what they want. The reason clients are on Elance is to get work done. Understand what they want, then let them know you "get it." When you've done that, you've most likely made a connection with them. This single step will put you in the top third of the pack.

You will still have to battle the fact that you don't have the feedback and ratings yet, but you're closer. You will find those clients who are looking for quality and are willing to give you that first yes.

Promoting Your Strengths

Until you get experience on Elance, you will be relying on your proposals and profile to get business. This will work fine, it just takes a bit longer. The key is to show how your strengths fit neatly into the job requirements.

Although you will always be promoting your strengths as you market your freelancing business, you have to do more of it yourself in the beginning. You don't have as much free advertising in the form of the feedback page.

As a new contractor, you have three main avenues for marketing yourself. Think of it as three legs to a stool:

- The proposal
- Your profile
- Communication in the bidding process

Within each of these you have more goodies, like specialties, references, work experience, training, etc. But you must view each of these steps as marketing opportunities, and they are interwoven like a fine rug. Use the following ideas to promote your strengths in any or all of the three avenues. Be creative, and above all else, fill the client's need.

Emphasize Your Profile

If you haven't built yourself a stellar profile yet, go back and read Chapter 4. You need this to get going. Your stool will tip right over if you don't have this important tool in place.

The proposal gets the prospective client's attention, and the profile keeps it. The sale is made between those two and your responses and questions in the bidding process. (See Chapter 5 for more steps to take to get noticed after you've submitted your proposal, and before the job has been awarded.)

Be sure to ask your prospective client to have a look at your profile. Tell them the truth: you're new to Elance but have an enormous amount of whatever it takes to get the job done.

TOP TIPS

Emphasizing your strengths is a fine balance. You want to showcase your talents, but you don't want to put people off by being too pushy. Stick with the facts presented in a clear and confident manner.

If you've taken care to really establish your profile and emphasize your strengths, this will impress the client. Be sure to include the personal touches, like a picture and/or YouTube video, to help create a connection.

Your profile is a selling tool. Use it as such. Getting the client to view it will help you make the sale.

Special Talents

Each of us has had unique experiences in our lives. Most of these have taught us valuable lessons, and we have all ended up with special talents along the way. Some are more obvious than others. Many people have special training in an area, or have spent years doing something in a traditional job that can easily be morphed into freelancing.

If you were a graphic designer in the military for 20 years, that will stand out well in your side career as a freelance 3D animator. It might not be exactly the same, but it's close and you should emphasize it.

However, maybe you're a CPA in a large firm, and your real desire is to become a travel writer. Obviously, emphasize any writing you've done in the past, including courses you've taken and publications you've had. But working as a CPA you also understand deadlines, overtime (think the weeks before April 15), and following through on quite important responsibilities to the client. These are critical for publishers.

The point is that you have special talents. Recognize what they are, dust them off and shine them up, and put them on display.

Ben Gran is a successful writer on Elance. He began with a single $200 writing project and has since earned over $100,000. He's a big believer in using a variety of work experiences to showcase your skills. In his words:

> "Think back on all your career experience and find ways to make it relevant to the various Elance jobs. I've used everything in my professional background to help find clients on Elance. I'm fortunate to be able to be versatile and flexible."

Ben's experience and success are an excellent example of using special talents. (You can find him on Elance under the user name Benjamin Gran.)

Past Experiences

You may not have any feedback or ratings on Elance, but you have your lifetime of experience. As with your specialties, use this information. It seems obvious to say, yet some contractors underestimate the value of what they've done in the past.

Direct job experience in your freelancing field is obviously going to help. Post this up front and center in your profile.

But as with specialties, many experiences highlight positive qualities that you just need to point out. Going through a rigorous training course proves that you stick with it when the going gets tough. Learning a second language means that you had a crash course in grammar, and also that you have a deeper level of understanding in that language's culture.

Ask yourself which of your experiences you can apply as positive attributes to your freelancing career. Again, a fine balance exists. Don't exaggerate or get crazy ideas about the talents your ant farm brings to the table, but do understand that you may have more experiences worth showcasing than you think you do.

Eager to Succeed

This one factor is sometimes the key ingredient that brings home the bacon. As a new contractor you have the desire and need to succeed. Tell this to your potential client right up front. Don't be shy about it. It's a matter of taking what's perceived to be a disadvantage—new on Elance—and turning it into an advantage.

TOP TIPS

Many clients will start a new contractor off with a test project. They may hire you for a small job to see how you do and how easy you are to work with. Run with these opportunities. Showcase your talent and professionalism, do a little extra and communicate frequently, while also maintaining the healthy boundaries you need for a balanced lifestyle.

When the client understands that you understand her project goal, that you are qualified to achieve it, and that you're hungry for the business and positive feedback, you become an attractive hire indeed. The key is to get all these pieces together.

Being eager to succeed is good, coming across as desperate is not. Bid your project fee appropriately, promptly follow up on any communication received, and let them know you understand what they want. Then do it again and again with potential jobs. This is eager but not desperate.

Follow Up

If a client asks specific questions in his job posting, answer them. Full stop. Just do it. Some clients will place questions in their postings just to filter out the boilerplate proposals from the real ones. If they get a response that answers the question, that contractor makes the A list. If the question isn't answered, that contractor gets the D-for-delete list.

As I mentioned in Chapter 5, send a follow-up email the same day or the day after you submit your proposal. In this email you can simply say the truth—you're following up because you're interested in the project. You can also add a relevant question or idea you've thought of in the meantime. The point is, you're in front of the prospective client twice in a short amount of time.

Next, you must wait; otherwise you can come across as desperate or just a pain in the backside. But if they respond to your proposal and/ or follow-up email—and they will if they're interested—respond promptly! If they're in touch with you, it's because they're interested. Everything you do is being judged, so see these moments for the opportunities they are.

Many clients are looking for long-term contractor relationships. The first jobs you do with them establish how well you work together. Following up on what you say you're going to do is key.

Communicate!

This one word can't be emphasized enough. If you have a question, ask. If you're asked a question, respond. Don't dally around wondering if the timing is right. Clear communication will help you win more jobs than perhaps any other quality.

> **CYBER SNAGS**
>
> If you're working from a much different time zone than your prospective client, be sure to mention this. This way she will understand when you respond at 3 A.M. her time, but are silent during normal working hours.

Time and again clients say that those contractors they are most likely to award the job to clearly communicate that they understand the project and are excellent at follow-up. Listen carefully to these words of wisdom.

Do the Hustle: The Numbers Game

At the end of the day, if you abide by all these bits of advice, and I hope you do, you will still have to submit many more proposals than you are awarded jobs for. It's a numbers game. At the beginning, you will be rejected more than you are accepted. Dust off your ego and get on with it.

When I first started my career as a freelancer, I promised myself I would submit two proposals a day. And I did. Twenty days later, this meant I had quite a lot of proposals out there. Eventually it paid off.

I never worried about all my proposals getting awarded at once; it didn't work that way for me. You may swing between way too much work and not enough, but over time you will find the balance. At the start, ya gotta hustle.

Most Common Pitfalls

Each of us has our unique quirks and foibles; however, common pitfalls exist that consistently trip up new contractors. In short, don't do the following:

- Give up too soon
- Take rejection personally
- Send out boilerplate proposals in the hope someone will take pity on you
- Have only one proposal out at a time
- Be slack on the quality or speed of your responses
- Skip over client questions in the job posting or otherwise
- Forget to communicate clearly that you understand the project needs
- Underestimate the value of your life experiences

The Subject of Underbidding

Underbidding is used far too often as a ploy to get awarded projects. As I mentioned previously, many top clients are actually put off by bids that come in too low. Other clients, however, have price as a main criteria for hiring. These people consistently hire the lowest bidder and there's not much you can do about it.

The question is, do you really want to work for someone who values cost above everything else? Is this the type of relationship you want? You provide a valuable service and should be able to charge appropriately. If you're not scoring those first, valuable jobs, then look into how you're marketing yourself before you consider lowering your fees to the bottom of the range.

Deliver, Deliver, Deliver

Once you get that first job on Elance, don't get all relaxed and gooey. Now's when you must deliver the goods above and beyond what the client expected. Don't slow down. They placed their trust in you when they clicked the green **Select** button. To get that crucial feedback, you must now shine.

> **CYBER SNAGS**
>
> After you've been awarded your first job, you may think it'll be easy from now on. But in reality, you must continue to submit many proposals and market yourself continuously until you get to a level where referrals and repeat projects keep your boat afloat. This will happen over time. Trust in the process.

After all, this is the fun part. You finally get to work in your new freelancing role. In order to develop repeat business and referrals, you must remember to deliver great service and quality work with each client. Don't let up just because the jobs are starting to come in. (Review Chapter 7 for ideas about delivering above-par service.)

Ask for Great Feedback

At the beginning of every project, and sometimes in the proposal itself, let the client know you're working for positive feedback. Get the subject right out in the open. As a new contractor, you need to build up this valuable sales tool, and sometimes all it takes is asking for it.

At the end of the project, bring up the subject again. Make sure they're completely satisfied with the job first, then ask them directly to give you stellar feedback. When they've done that, thank them.

Keep At It!

Success takes time, and sometimes you'll need to remind yourself of that. At the beginning it can seem like you'll never get a job, or that the ones you're getting will always be small and you'll never get the repeat business you want. Kick those thoughts right out of your mind.

You do have what it takes and you do have something to offer. Remind yourself of that as often as necessary. Print it out and tape it on your favorite child's forehead. You'll never have to worry about a large percentage of your competition because they're the ones who gave up. Don't join that party.

Stay away from negative people who want to drag you down. You don't need that burden on top of everything else. Let them wallow in their misery, while you go right on submitting proposals. Think of it as a game, you're putting together the pieces of a puzzle and when you get it right, you are awarded a job and get paid for it.

The Least You Need to Know

- You have what it takes to be a successful freelancer.
- With each new project, you're building feedback as a valuable sales tool.
- Use your special talents and life experiences to help promote yourself.
- Good follow-up is critical.
- When the client is satisfied with the end result, ask for great feedback.
- Those who stick with it win.

Growing Your Business as an Elance Client

This part is devoted to Elance clients looking to hire the best talent possible. However, as the previous part was for contractors but helpful for clients as well, the same logic applies here. Contractors should read this part so they will understand how the client thinks and what they experience.

The client will learn how they are actually competing for the best contractors online and therefore how to present themselves to attract this talent. I also discuss how the client can target top contractors by studying their profiles, track records, and portfolios of sample work.

The client's job is also to craft detailed job postings so contractors know they're working with a serious and professional employer. I show clients how to do this and include examples of both good and bad postings. Choosing the right person to hire includes not only researching his information, but also taking into account how he or she communicates during the selection process. I provide best practices for how to proactively discover the highest-quality contractors out of many choices.

The part concludes with a chapter devoted to how the Elance platform enables the online work experience. The widgets, gadgets, and add-ons all serve to make sure your virtual office runs smoothly. I finish with concrete steps to nurture the client-contractor connection and therefore build long-term working relationships.

Attracting the Best— The Client Image

In This Chapter

- Assessing your image as an Elance client
- Using your profile as a self-advertising tool
- Understanding the freelancer universe
- Seeing yourself from the contractors' eyes

As you begin your journey hiring talent on Elance, just like a contractor does, you need to stop and carefully assess what image you're showcasing in this online work world. Presenting yourself as a professional isn't just for contractors seeking work. You, as a potential client, and as you search for talented freelancers across the globe, need to consider your business persona.

The number and quality of freelancers available is rising. Equally, more and more jobs are being posted and their depth and complexity is expanding. This means the virtual work world is coming into its own, and clients need to stand out as professionals in order to attract the best hires. Competition not only exists amongst contractors, but amongst clients as well.

In this chapter, you will learn how to present yourself online to attract the best talent. Your online image speaks volumes to potential contractors. By tailoring this image and understanding what it is contractors are looking for, you can save time and money in appealing to the best talent the web has to offer.

The Key to Top Talent

One of the single most important aspects that you, as a client, must remember is that the best talent is also assessing and evaluating you. In later chapters I will show you how to search for freelancers for your job, and I will explain how to write effective job descriptions (in Chapters 10 and 11, respectively).

However, you'll be carving the turkey with a dull knife if you don't also consider how they will see you in return. The best contractors are very busy people. Some will be available on the spot, if your timing is good. And others will let you know if they have time, and if so when it would be. In return, you will get some very high-quality work done.

So before you begin your search for the best talent, and before you design your magnetic job posting, you need to sit back and understand how you are viewed by those you want to hire. Learn what they will see and value. Doing this is time well spent.

The Client Profile

The best freelancers are going to assess your history with Elance. They have learned through experience that not all clients are easy or desirable to work for. Just as you have red and green flags in finding great contractors, they in turn will have the same for you. As with so many aspects of success, through knowledge you can turn this into an advantage.

CYBER SNAGS

Contractors are on the watch for unprofessional clients. Nobody likes their time wasted or their talent unappreciated. Only post projects when you know what you want and are ready to hire someone and get going.

After reading your job posting, the contractor will check out your profile if interested. A couple of ways are available to do this.

Two Views Top Talent Will Use

If a contractor has been searching for jobs through the search mechanism, they can easily get a quick scan of your statistics from the thumbnail job posting.

To view client statistics as in Figure 9.1, click on **Find Work** on the main toolbar. This will bring up the Job Search page that contractors use to find projects.

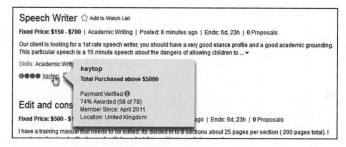

Figure 9.1: *A glimpse of a client's statistics can be seen directly from the job search results.*

In the bottom-left corner of each project, you will find a series of four dots, some will be green, along with the user name and location of the client. Hover your cursor over the dots or the client's name. A box appears with basic client information.

In Figure 9.1, you can see that the total purchased by this client is over $5,000. This gives them four green dots and is an easy way for contractors to spot potentially active clients. Payment verified means the client's method of payment has been verified by Elance and is ready to go. Contractors like this.

The percentage of jobs awarded is a closely watched statistic by contractors. If the ratio is low, it means this client might not be serious and might be a waste of time. Big red flag. The data also shows how long the client has been a member of Elance and where he is located.

Next, click on the client's user name. Now their actual profile will appear. Most important for the contractor are the statistics and the feedback. Obviously, when you first join Elance you won't have any data, but over time you will and this is what the talent you're searching for will see.

To find your own profile, hover your cursor over **Hire** in the main top toolbar. In the drop-down menu, click on **Client Profile**. This brings up your Client Profile page.

What are contractors looking for? Initially, an active client, as shown by the total number of jobs posted, a high award ratio, and a larger dollar amount of total projects purchased. They want you to be active and serious. If you're not that active, that's okay, but you must place more emphasis on your job posting (see Chapter 11).

Next, your feedback to other contractors will be reviewed. See Figure 9.2 for what the Feedback section looks like. Contractors are checking for clients with consistently high ratings and positive written feedback. This means you're probably professional and good to work for. They will read what you've written and what type of relationships you've developed. They will read what the hired contractor says about you in return.

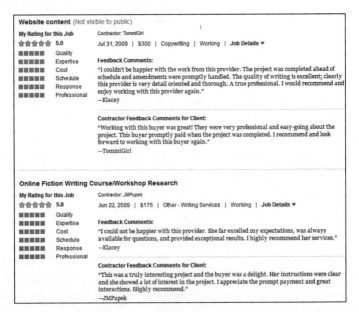

Figure 9.2: *Client and contractor feedback is viewed by contractors to see what type of work experiences you've had already on Elance.*

For great clients who post quality jobs, the feedback area is free advertising. Equally, contractors will notice if projects consistently don't go well or seem troubled in some way. The message here isn't to fiddle with the statistics, you can't. It's that if you're a good client, part of the work of attracting top talent is done for you right here. This is true self-advertising to attract top Elance talent.

Profile Extras

As a client, you also have the ability to showcase yourself and/or your company. This is another way to let the contractor know you're serious about your projects on Elance. In Figure 9.3, the client has written a brief description about his company and the services they provide.

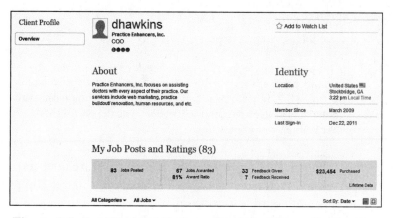

Figure 9.3: *Providing a brief company description on your client profile is another way to show you're serious.*

You also have the ability to upload a company logo or photograph, and you can post a YouTube video. These are great ways to begin making the connection necessary for long-term, quality working relationships. It's not just clients that want to hire the best, but the best talent wants to work for professional clients. By using these tools, you are able to hone your image and attract top talent.

The Freelancer Universe

One of the magical qualities about hiring in the virtual work world is your amazing access to talent. The freelancer universe is deep and wide and jam-packed full of potential. These talented individuals are online for the sole purpose of finding quality work. Whatever their motivation—laid off, career change, haunted by a dream, work while the kids are at school—their goal now is to take on freelancing projects.

However, given the irascible laws of nature, not all of these talented people will make it. For whatever reason, the 80–20 rule applies to online hires. Eighty percent of the talent will arrive for a while and then gradually fade away. But the twenty percent that remains will achieve success and hopefully work for you.

> **BEST PRACTICES**
>
> In the beginning, you won't have the free advertising provided by the feedback and statistics that other clients have. Don't worry, you can overcome this by being clear, honest, and easy to communicate with. Contractors develop a second sense about who the best clients are, just like clients do with contractors.

In the next chapter, I will give you specific steps to search out and invite specific contractors to bid on your projects. But first, it's important to understand not only how broad a field you have to choose from, but also how the best are in demand. It's your job to not only find them, but to get them as interested in you as you are in them.

Like Attracts Like

As with so many things in life, when hiring online you get what you ask for. The issue is, some of us don't realize what it is we just asked for. Our image and actions communicate as much as or more than the meaning conveyed by our actual words. Because of this, it's crucial that we understand what we're expressing when online.

If you present a sloppy and ill-thought-out persona, that's who you'll find when your job proposals start coming in. If you're only interested in finding the cheapest contractor possible, at the sacrifice of quality, well, you can count on it then. And if you're looking for quality working relationships, where the job progresses flawlessly, well, you must do your part to make sure that's what you're attracting.

Not to worry. It's easy. Let's start with what you look like right now.

A Look in the Mirror

So if this image of yours is all important, the first thing you need to do is step back and have a look at it. You understand the value of the profile, and later, in Chapter 11, you'll learn how to communicate what you want done in a clear and effective way. In the meantime, there are yet more ways you can communicate who you are.

First Impressions

The key here is to think about what you want from Elance and how you're going to go about getting it, before you barge right in and slap your money down on the bar. Most of you will probably be testing the waters to see if you like this new way of doing business. To get the best results, you need to manage that first impression.

CYBER SNAGS

When using email as a main source of communication, be aware of how you may be coming across. Capital letters make it LOOK LIKE YOU'RE SHOUTING, when perhaps that's not the message you intended. Humor doesn't always come across right because you don't have the facial expressions (like a smile) and body language to accentuate the story.

Start with focusing specifically on what you want to get done and make it small. You may have heard success stories about start-ups built solely with Elance freelancers—and these stories are true and abound—but put a toe in first so you understand how things work.

What you don't want to do is throw yourself in headfirst, make some mistakes that you could have avoided, and then end up with a bad taste and/or bad feedback. Start slowly. Learn. And organize that first impression so attracting the best contractors will come naturally.

Spelling Counts

If English isn't your first language, or even if it wasn't your best subject in school, learn about Spell Check. It's easy to use, really. The devil is in the details. Manage these and they add to your overall image.

Another alternative is to hire a proofreader on Elance. These folks get paid to make sure you come across grammatically intact. Hire someone to proof your job postings, your profile blurb, whatever. But make sure your written word is professional looking.

Clarity

Clarity isn't just reserved for job postings. Whenever you communicate with a contractor, prospective or not, be as clear and precise as possible. One top client claims he always writes to a fifth grade level. This isn't to say anyone isn't intelligent. It's to say be clear. You might be working with someone on the other side of the world where language is an issue.

BEST PRACTICES

Clients with businesses should take the time to explain the business as a whole to the contractor. Each smaller project is part of the greater whole and by understanding this end vision, each piece can be more accurate.

As I mention so many times in this book, communication is key. If your instructions are vague, so goes your response, and perhaps, so goes your project, too. When you're first communicating with contractors to determine whether they're a fit, it's especially important to communicate clearly. They don't want to muddle through an unclear project or client, and the best simply won't.

Job History

By starting small and communicating clearly, your job history—that all-important self-advertising—will take care of itself. The feedback you leave will most probably be positive, as will the comments your contractors leave for you. By setting things up right from the beginning, you will attract the best and make sure you leave a good trail behind you. It's not that hard to do.

Proactive Attraction

Top clients agree on the best things you can do to attract and keep quality talent. These can be distilled down into several key points:

- Remember that you are competing for talent.
- Always be professional, yet personable.
- Communicate clearly at all times.
- Be honest in what you are asking for.
- Don't be cheap. You will reap what you sow.
- Create positive work experiences which will lead to excellent feedback comments.
- Explain your overall business vision and how it relates to the project at hand.

These steps aren't difficult, and the results they produce are well worth the effort.

The Least You Need to Know

- It's crucial to understand that you are competing for talent.
- Contractors will view your client profile and statistics.
- You have a world of talent to choose from and need to attract the best.
- The message you send determines the type and quality of contractor in return.
- Understand what's important to a contractor.
- Use proactive steps to let contractors know you're serious.

Targeting Top Talent

In This Chapter

- Clarifying your project
- Categories and skill sets
- The keyword search
- Advanced search parameters
- Posting your job
- Inviting contractors

Meeting great contractors on Elance doesn't have to be a matter of sitting back and hoping the right person finds and bids on your project. While this passive method might work, you can also take a more proactive approach to searching for the perfect fit. You can post your project to the entire Elance universe, you can invite select contractors, or you can do both.

Elance also takes part in the talent search by matching contractors with you that they feel might fit your project's specifications and your job history. These are presented in an easy-to-view format for you to add to your list of choices.

This chapter will show you how to identify contractors that just might fit the bill by focusing your project and using Elance's search tools. It's a matter of understanding what you have to choose from, and then how to find the contractors within these groups.

Focus Your Project

An important and commonsense aspect within the search process is often overlooked: make sure you know exactly what it is you want done in your job. Sounds strange? You'd be surprised just how many clients have a pretty good idea of what they want done, but in fact it's vague enough that the selection of contractors who bid is far too wide. Or they're unclear exactly what the project parameters are and time is wasted in clarification.

> **BEST PRACTICES**
>
> As you clarify in your mind what you want done in your project, also leave room for the contractors' ideas and creativity. They're the experts for good reason, and as you search you will get a feel for those who have the style you're looking for.

This doesn't mean you have to be an expert in the job itself. After all, if you're hiring someone to build your website it could be because you don't have the time, or, more likely, it's because you simply don't know how to do it well enough to take it on yourself. That's why we hire people!

Focusing your project means identifying the end result as clearly as possible. I'll go over how to explain this step-by-step in Chapter 11. But first, you need to have this end result in mind when you begin to target contractors.

If you're thinking you want to have a website built to help you increase business, that's great. But it's vague. If it's for business, do you want it search engine optimized? You may not have a clue about how to do that, but you may now want a contractor that can both build the website and do the SEO. Or you may want to hire two, one for each aspect of the project.

Will you be selling widgets directly from your site? It doesn't matter if you know how to set this up, you just need to know that you want it.

If you're looking for a virtual assistant, make a list of all the areas in which you need help organizing. If you need an iPhone app designed, understand who the end users will be and how they will apply the tool. By solidifying your project in your mind even before you write the job posting, you will have better luck as you search through contractors to target.

Contractor Categories

As you've seen already, you have several general categories to choose from when searching for a contractor. For the most part, it's pretty clear which category you'll be searching within. However, sometimes you're not sure. Is it Sales and Marketing that you're looking for, or Design and Multimedia?

BEST PRACTICES

As you begin sifting through the wonderful world of contractors, you'll come across many that are of interest. Elance has a handy Watch List feature next to each contractor's profile. Use this or you can end up searching for ages for that one great contractor you ran across but just can't find again.

To help narrow your choices, you can actually search for specific skills within each category. Click on **Hire** in the top left of the main toolbar. This will bring up a drop-down menu. Click on **Browse** to reach the categories shown in Figure 10.1.

Categories | Skills

Programmers	**Designers**	**Writers**
Web	Graphic	Articles
Software	Logo	Web Content
Mobile	Illustration	Blogs
SEO	Animation	Translations
Blogs	Brochures	Copywriting
Database	Banners	Technical Writing
QA	Presentations	Ghostwriting
Other	Other	Other

Marketers	**Admins**	**Consultants**
Advertising	Customer Service	Accounting
SEM - Search Engine	Virtual Assistance	Finance
SMM - Social Media	Data Entry	Engineering
Sales & Lead Gen	Web Research	Legal
Telemarketing	Email Handling	Product Design
Email	Transcription	Human Resources
Research & Surveys	Word Processing	Management
Other	Other	Other

Figure 10.1: *Within each category are subsets of skills. These can help you target contractors.*

When you click on one of the individual skills, you'll be taken to the page listing all contractors registered with that skill. Contractors may appear within more than one category skill. And of course, you may need more than one skill for your job. This gives you a direct way to search for those skills.

Target Your Contractor

Now we get into the meat of the issue. You know to get a clear picture of what elements you need covered in your project, and you understand which categories and skill subsets you have to choose from.

Searching for contractors within a specific category and the even narrower skill set will distill the quantity down to those who emphasize what you're looking for. But then what? Under the category of Design and Multimedia, and within the subset skill of Graphic, you still have more than 52,000 contractors to choose from. Not something you might want to sit down and scroll through in an afternoon. But you can reduce this amount of prospects yet further.

Keywords

By using keywords, you're able to refine your search to a specific skill or a combination of them. Just like when you're searching for something on Google or another search engine, you type in the keyword or phrase that applies in the search box at the top of the page. With keywords you can narrow your focus to those top contractors with the skill sets you're looking for.

CYBER SNAGS

When using keywords to search for your contractors, remember to keep them simple and precise. Don't say "website with music and videos." Rather, type in just the basic words, "website music video." Try it and see the difference.

Individuals vs. Companies

You can filter for this differentiation through the Elance system. On the top-left side of your Contractor Search page, you'll find a menu titled Narrow Results. The very first item is the choice between filtering for Individuals or Companies. If you click on **Individuals**, you can then choose from those who are Independent or those who are Company Members.

Some clients want to work with individual contractors only. They believe they will get more attention and personal detail. Other clients like the benefits that come when working with a diverse array of people.

The key is to add this information into your total assessment. There is no fixed rule for what works best, but it's always better to be aware of your choices. Will you get lost in the whirl of a large company? Will you miss out on creative opportunities with a niche marketer? It depends on your project, and on your personality.

Specialists vs. Generalists

Some contractors promote narrow fields of expertise; others strive to cover many possible needs in the same general category. Let's say you want a professional resume built. Elance is the perfect place to come shop for freelancers to do just this.

Type in your keyword, **Resume**. Up comes a selection of over 12,000 contractors with resume in their profile keyword list. Here you'll see on the first page alone you have the choice between specialists and generalists.

For example, a contractor called Advanced Resume Writing has nearly made a sweet $20,000 this year. With a more thorough search of her profile, you'll see that resume writing is, indeed, the only service she offers. Consider this in your search of contractors. Remember, later in this chapter I'll show you how to invite specific contractors to your job posting.

Other contractors in this same search, however, provide a wider array of services. Consider First Rate Consulting, which claims, "Expert Resume Writer/Career Development Specialist/Human Resources Professional." In the world of helping a client advance in his or her career, this contractor is much more of a generalist.

Either of these freelancers might write you a great, job-winning resume. But it's important to add these additional factors into your overall search results. It comes right back to focus, this time not just your own but the contractor's, too.

The Search Sort

As you search for contractors, you'll notice a long menu on the left side of the main screen. This is a treasure chest of wonderful tools for narrowing down your contractor search. The purpose of searching for contractors isn't to narrow your selection to the one best individual or business for the job. Rather, you want to create a short list of those you will specifically invite to submit a proposal. And keep in mind when sorting that a short list doesn't have to be short. It's all relative. Don't think you need to choose only a set few contractors to invite. You can make your short list as long as you like. The idea is to identify those specific individuals or businesses you feel might be best and invite them.

Over time, you'll learn which search filters are more applicable to you and what you're looking for. But I'll run through the most important so you get the idea.

Categories and Tested Skills

On the top of the left menu, choose which category you want to search within. Click on subcategories to further narrow your results.

Tested skills are based on tests Elance contractors have taken to determine where they rank in that skill compared to other Elancers. Over 300 skill tests have been designed by Elance and taking them is completely voluntary. Beware, the contractor can post the actual result from the test, or post a "self-rated" score. The latter is of questionable value as it's the contractor posting an imaginary result.

Location

You can also narrow your search by location, as shown in Figure 10.2. For those clients who want to meet face-to-face with their contractor, or for those who only want contractors from certain global geographic regions, this is your go-to spot.

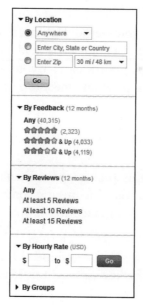

Figure 10.2: *Elance provides several different ways to search for contractors.*

If you believe the best IT services come out of India, you can narrow this here. Perhaps you have a document written in English that you want translated into Mandarin Chinese. Choose **Eastern Asia** from the drop-down menu, and the system will only bring up contractors from that area.

Features like this truly underline how effective the global workplace is. No longer are we strictly bound by borders and languages. Your specific project can be done by a talented freelancer from most anywhere in the world. Keep this in mind as you create your short list of contractors.

CYBER SNAGS

In order for a contractor to designate himself from a specific location, business must be conducted from the country specified in the sign up process. However, that doesn't prevent the contractor from farming out the business to other regions of the world. If you're unsure, ask where and by whom the work actually gets done. Elance is working to close these technological loopholes.

You can also search for contractors within a fixed-mile radius of where you live. If you're not completely ready for hiring that talented logo designer from the Ukraine, narrow your location search results to within where you can drive and meet for a coffee. The choice is yours.

Feedback

This is one of the most useful sort tools. Feedback refers to what other clients have said about this specific contractor's service. Using the five-star rating system, Elance allows you to sort for those with the highest average rating (as you can see back in Figure 10.2).

At first flush, this seems like a no-brainer. Of course you want to sort by those with the highest ratings! But remember that this may place contractors with fewer, albeit perfect, rankings higher up the list. The more projects a contractor takes on, the more likelihood that he will eventually receive lower ratings. It's just the way it works. So an excellent contractor may appear lower down the line simply because he had more time to get beaten up in the real world.

Reviews, Hourly Rates, and Groups

These final parameters have their uses. The Reviews option allows you to include only those contractors with a set number of reviews into your search results. This eliminates new or relatively new contractors. Remember, some of the best opportunities lay with hardworking newcomers who want to prove their stuff. But if that's not what you want, you can filter it out here.

Hourly Rates are just that. You can search for contractors that provide services with certain hourly rates.

The Groups filter sorts for those contractors who belong to Elance groups. These are alliances sponsored by companies or organizations and have certain membership requirements. They are voluntary to join and over 80 exist. The eligibility is determined by the sponsor, not Elance.

The Cumulative Effect

One interesting aspect to this sorting process is that the filters work together. As you add search parameters, you end up with several layers of filtering, as shown in Figure 10.3.

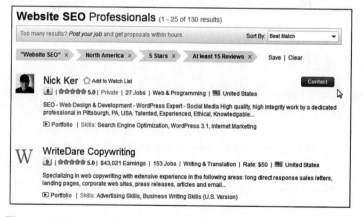

Figure 10.3: *This Website SEO example shows several layers of search parameters working cumulatively.*

Let's say you wanted the SEO content for your website written by a freelancer. Because your company is in the United States, you want a native English speaker to do the writing. So you add North America as a location parameter.

Next, you only want those contractors with a five-star average rating, and only those with 15 ratings of this level or more. Voilà, you have 130 contractors who fit this bill. That's still a lot to choose from, but you've narrowed it down and have incorporated valuable parameters.

Don't Overlook the Newbie

At one time, all of us were new at something we were passionate about and qualified to do. Yet because we hadn't built up an impressive resume and didn't have references bursting to sing our praises, we missed out on opportunities that we could have done well.

The same holds true for new Elance contractors. When they come up in your search results, don't just scan right past. Give them a chance. In some cases, they'll work harder and longer for you than a more seasoned freelancer will.

> **CYBER SNAGS**
>
> One of the drawbacks of sorting for contractors is you might miss out on the newbie opportunity. One way to make sure you get proposals from them is to not solely invite selected contractors. Leave the job posting open to all Elancers, and the up-and-coming stars will find you.

After all, they have everything to lose. One bad rating at the beginning can destroy a budding career. They're well aware of this and will work hard to avoid it. You may need to have a little more patience as they learn the system, but there's a lot of great talent out there. Elance is growing fast and new contractors are coming online all the time. Don't miss out.

Posting Your Job

Many links exist on the Elance system where you can post your job. The most common and useful is to simply click on **Hire** in the upper-left corner of the main toolbar. Then click **Post a Job**.

Crafting effective job descriptions is so important that I've devoted an entire chapter to it (see Chapter 11). So here I'll just go through the nuts and bolts of how to post, who to post to, and what to watch out for.

Nuts and Bolts

The basics for posting a job are pretty straightforward. I'll go through it step by step:

1. Give your job a name and make it short and specific. This is what contractors will see and decide to bid on or not. You want to clearly explain the nut of what you want done.

> **BEST PRACTICES**
>
> I once saw a job posting titled "Read check up." Confusing to say the least. I still haven't figured it out. But the posting right below said, "Create five blog topics and outlines." Clarity is key and will get you the best prospective contractors.

2. The Describe It area is where you give the details of your job. Again, I'll go over this in the next chapter.

3. Choose the category of work. This will determine which set of contractors can bid on your project. A contractor who works under Finance and Management cannot bid on projects under Sales and Marketing, for example. You can also select one subcategory from within the main category. This will help contractors with that specific skill set find your job.

4. In **Request specific skills or groups**, you can select five additional skills you're looking for. This helps when contractors use keywords to search for projects to bid on.

5. Choose **Hourly** or **Fixed price**, as shown in Figure 10.4. Then pick an estimated hourly range, or an estimated fixed price for your job. Contractors can bid higher or lower, but this gives them an idea of what you're thinking. It also tells them how serious you are. Top contractors will not work for the lowest wages. They understand the value they bring.

6. Click on **Privacy and other options**. This brings up an extra screen where you have some interesting choices.

7. Choose the job location (if relevant), the number of days you want the project posted on Elance for, and if you want your chosen contractor to begin immediately.

8. Finally, in **Job posting visibility**, you get to choose if you want to open up your project to all contractors within your category, or if you just want to invite select contractors. You can also do both by opening the project to the Elance public, but then inviting specific contractors after you've posted the job. I recommend the latter as you'll get the most choices.

9. Click **Continue** to review and post the job. **Save and post later** will save your posting but not make it public until you give the go-ahead.

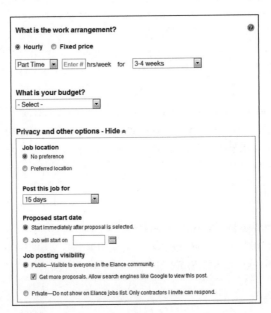

Figure 10.4: *Work arrangement options when posting a job.*

You will also have the opportunity to post a featured job. This highlights the proposal with the intent of attracting more contractor bids. Because it costs $30, it shows you're that much more serious.

Inviting Contractors

You can easily invite contractors to bid on your project. Go back and click on **Hire** at the top left of the main toolbar. Click on **Search Contractors**. This takes you back to the search page.

Type in the name of the contractor you want to hire. In the results you will notice a green Contact button in the top-right corner (see Figure 10.5). Click on this and you can either invite them to any current job posting you have open or create a new posting that will automatically invite them.

Figure 10.5: *Click on the green **Contact** button to invite this contractor to submit a proposal to your job.*

After you've clicked on the **Contact** button, a pop-up box like in Figure 10.6 will appear. Here you have the option to invite this contractor to an existing job or you can create a new job posting.

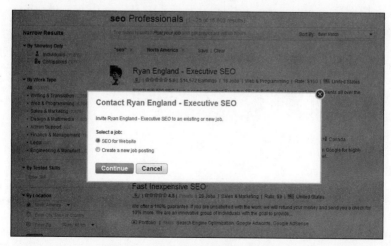

Figure 10.6: *Inviting a contractor.*

Elance Search Results

When you have posted your job, Elance itself will provide you with suggested contractors to choose from (as shown in Figure 10.7). They base these potential matches on the parameters of your job posting, as well as your history of jobs. In the latter, they analyze the parameters you normally hire within and include these.

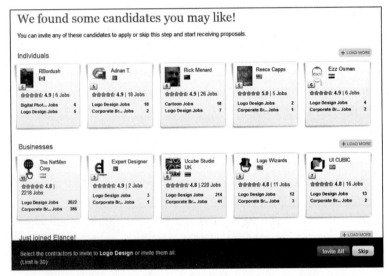

Figure 10.7: *Potential contractor matches selected by Elance.*

The search matches will be grouped into individuals, businesses, new Elance contractors, and, when possible, they will include those contractors that are based near you geographically.

To invite a contractor from these matches, just click on the square profile and they will be automatically shifted to a list of invitees. You can also choose to invite them all (within limits based on your paying membership level).

The Least You Need to Know

- Focus your job so you are clearer on the skills you need.
- Use the advanced search parameters.
- Search parameters are cumulative to help you really drill down.
- Don't overlook the opportunities with new contractors.
- Posting a job is quick and easy.
- Open up your job posting to all Elance contractors in your category, but also invite those that stood out in your search.
- Check out the contractor matches Elance has selected for you.

Laserlike Job Postings

In This Chapter

- The single most important quality in a job posting
- Becoming clear about your project goals
- What a sample job posting looks like
- What top contractors are looking for
- A posting structure to follow

Learning how to post effective job descriptions is key to success as a client on Elance or any other online hiring site. The first reason for this is obvious; your prospective freelancer will have a clear understanding of what you want from your job. Through understanding your goals, they will be able to meet them.

The second reason is no less important but less commonly thought of. Through your posting you are communicating what type of client you will be to work for. Top contractors know this and watch carefully. Yes, they want to win jobs and make money, but not at the expense of working for someone who is unclear and impossible to please.

Fortunately, writing concise and upbeat job postings is easy to learn and clearly covered in this chapter. By clarifying your goals and distilling them down to the essentials, you will be able to save time and money in your online job quest. Read on!

It Boils Down to ...

Consistently, Elance top clients agree the key to effective job descriptions boils down to one word: Clarity. The more clear and precise they make their postings, the better the quality of proposals in their inbox. Attention paid to this single aspect of their project reaps huge rewards in both the hiring process and in the end result because they've attracted the best to choose from.

If you are not clear in your description you will end up with a more scattered selection of contractors bidding. This isn't to say you'll end up with subpar freelancers, but you may end up with those that don't understand your needs well enough. They will either not give you targeted job proposals (how can they if they don't have a clear idea of your goals?), or they will specialize in the wrong areas. Or both.

Often, the single biggest mistake you can make when hiring on Elance is posting unclear job descriptions. This can simply lead to hiring the wrong people. It's no one's fault, it just points right back to communicating clearly.

If you post laserlike job descriptions, you will automatically increase the efficiency of the freelancers who respond. Let's look at how you can do this. (You will find more examples of job postings in Appendix B.)

Clarity Begins at Home

First and foremost, have a clear picture of what you want from your project. The clearer it is for you, the more detailed and helpful you will be able to write it in your description. Take some time and list as many features and aspects as you can. Initially, be overly detailed. Then you can tailor it back to streamline the actual posting.

BEST PRACTICES

As important as it is to clarify your project, it's also crucial to refine it so it's not too long. Pages of description can put contractors off and might flag you as a pain. Being concise is the key.

The point is not to inundate your prospective contractor with minutiae, but to be able to bullet point those precise features and qualities you're looking for. Each project will be different, but consider including the following:

- A clear description of the end result.

- What you will actually be using the project for so your contractor can place it into perspective. This might include a description of your business.

- A detailed list of any extra features you want included.

- Examples of similar products or services.

- A list of any specific contractor skills required and/or preferred.

- Questions for the contractor to determine what solutions they come up with, and to see how responsive they are to your specific job.

- Clear milestones along the way, if necessary.

- A deadline.

By outlining your needs in this fashion (and your list may vary), you are helping to focus your project for the benefit of the people who will be bidding on it. It's a matter of distilling your vision to the clearest possible core.

Let's dig a little deeper.

What's in a Name?

Giving your job an appropriate name is a surprisingly important aspect to the entire process. Contractors are searching for jobs on Elance 24/7. Each will have specialties they're looking to fulfill, and the easier you can make it to find you the better.

For example, let's say you want an app built for iPhones. You could title your job "iPhone App." Or you could be more specific, like "jQuery mobile app (v2)." Right off the bat, those contractors with expertise in jQuery version 2 mobile applications know to look deeper into your job posting.

Let's say you want a brochure made for your business. You could title your job "Brochure needed." Or you could help zero in on specific talent by titling it "Food brochure design, 15 pages." Immediately the contractor has a better idea of what you're looking for.

> **BEST PRACTICES**
>
> Building clear and concise postings doesn't just help you clarify your project goals. It also flags you as a good person to work for. Remember, you're also being judged by the best contractors.

Titling your project precisely is one more way you refine the communication process. Freelancers scrolling through their job searches can quickly identify projects they want to bid on by pinpointed titles. This saves everyone time.

The Nitty-Gritty

The same type of detail you apply to your job title needs to be applied within the posting as well. To use the previous example of the iPhone application, you could give a generic, albeit accurate, description of the end result:

> "Create an airline ticket application for iphones, ipads, and android devices."

Yes, it's giving a picture of the end result and what the client wants. However, compare that level of detail with the following:

> "Our budget for the first phase of this project is $900. A second phase will start in one month.
>
> FastFlight is a mobile airline ticket application. It allows people to easily find the cheapest flights, and to share their results with friends and family on social networks.
>
> We are looking for a developer who can code the mobile app with these technologies:

— jQuery Mobile
— HTML5
— CSS3
— JavaScript

Experience with Git is also a plus.

The app design is in a layered PSD file. You will extract images from the PSD file.

You will implement the mobile app UI, while a back-end developer will supply the JSON API.

Thank you!"

Which posting do you think will get the most specific bidders? It's this type of detail that will help you target and attract the best free-lancers. Their goal is to understand what you want and to give it to you in exchange for being paid money. The more you can help them understand your goals, the easier the entire project will flow.

Research

Sometimes you won't know all the details you need in your project. After all, you're not the expert; that's why you're hiring someone online. One way to overcome this is to research similar projects and see what they're asking for.

CYBER SNAGS

As you research ideas from similar job postings, be careful about making specific decisions without being fully informed. If necessary, Google technologies you don't understand and read up on what other people say about the latest trends. If you're still not sure what's best, you can always list the options in your posting and see what the contractors recommend.

Let's say you want a website built for your new business but you don't really know much more about it than that. Go to **Find Work** in the top main toolbar. Here you can search through other jobs that have been posted. On the left hand menu of categories, click on **IT & Programming**. In the subcategories list that will appear, click on **Website Design**.

Now you have in front of you the entire list of website design–related job postings on Elance. Scroll through and look for those that may be similar to yours. This is a great way to educate yourself as to what's out there, and to gain ideas for your own postings.

Maybe you see that one client is concerned about ensuring the artwork used for his website is copyright free. If this applies to you, make a note. It's astounding what you can learn by just having a cruise around this area. You can also see what clear and decidedly unclear job postings look like.

And If You Still Don't Know

In the end, if you still feel uncomfortable about the details in your posting, or if you simply don't have time to do the research necessary, ask the contractors. You're not expected to be the expert. If you are, that's great. But many clients need help finding the best solutions for their projects.

 CYBER SNAGS

Asking questions is a great way to gain information and establish rapport. But be careful: if you ask too many questions, or if they're way too simple, you can be flagged as indecisive by contractors. Apply the happy medium of not too hot and not too cold, but just right.

This approach has three distinct benefits. First, you'll get recommendations from some of the most talented freelancers in the world. There's nothing like going to the best for advice. Some contractors may be too busy to spend the time on someone who doesn't know what he's doing, but others will truly help you out.

Second, you'll learn very quickly which contractors actually read your proposal and take the time to address your needs specifically. Boilerplate bids are common and asking questions is a great way to see who's really thinking about you.

Third, by asking questions you establish rapport with your potential contractors. Very quickly you will learn who is responsive and clear, and who just can't be bothered to fill in the gaps. In no time at all, this will help you develop your short list of freelancers. Chapter 12 goes into this process in depth.

Pricing Your Project

Asking the right price for the work you need done is a crucial piece of the equation. If your price is too low, you'll eliminate top talent. However, if the price is too high, you'll be paying more than you should. Fortunately, you have a few options to help you out.

First, do some research. Search for jobs as if you were a contractor by clicking on **Hire**, then the appropriate subcategories on the left-side menu. See what other clients are asking for similar work. Be sure to note if they have lots of proposals coming in, or just a few.

Next, remember you have a range to work from. In both fixed-price and hourly jobs you can select quite a wide price range for the bids to fall within. This means you don't have to pick a specific price but can see what each contractor is willing to accept for their fee. If you're absolutely not sure what to charge, you can always choose **Not Sure**.

The key is to select a fair price range to work from and not try to get your work done for a ridiculously cheap price. "You get what you pay for" is sage advice here.

Sample Job Posting

The following is a sample job posting for a community college in need of a travel writing course. The description is clear, as are the use and goals. I've commented in bold on individual aspects.

We are a local community college and need a course written on "Travel Writing" that can be used for online education.

The final course must be 15,000 words divided into 12 concise lessons.

The posting starts with a clear summary of what is needed and for whom and what purpose.

The course should be written in a Word .doc file format on the topic of travel writing.

Goal: The goal of this course is to provide comprehensive information about travel writing and publication for a target market of any age individual.

The goal is clearly stated with the target market. This is of great help for the writer, as he will know what type of detail and vocabulary to use.

Details:

— Provide a lesson outline within one week for us to approve before you begin. Topics to include are listed at the bottom.

— The course must be 15,000 words divided into 12 lessons with copyright-free images.

— Quizzes: The end of each lesson must have 10 to 12 review questions in a multiple-choice format. (Highlight the correct answer for our instructional setup, and please provide the answer explanations for these.)

— Images: Any images used must be copyright free.

Do not use Wikipedia as a source.

Deadline: 30 days.

These details describe all the deliverable information and the deadline. The milestones are the outline in one week and the full course within 30 days.

Please include at least the following topics in the course:

— History of travel writing

— Equipment needed

— Inverted pyramid style

— Style manuals

— Getting published

— Targeting publishers

— Interview tips

— Finding the story that sells

To end with, the client posted specific subjects that should be covered but the contractor is not limited to just these.

More aspects or details could be included in such a proposal. But it's a great example of creating a clear description of what's needed without overwhelming the bidders with page after page of demands. It provides structure but allows for the creativity of the contractor to come through.

Elance Templates

Elance also helps with job postings by providing templates for standard job requests. For unique jobs, like in the previous example, these might not work as well, but for many jobs this is a good starting point. Your own previous job postings will be available to use as templates, too. All you need to do is go in and change the details.

Access Elance's templates from the job posting site itself. Click on the **Post Your Job** button and you will be taken to the page where you create your job posting.

Type in the name of your job and template choices will appear on the right, as shown in Figure 11.1. In this case, all I did was type in **Logo design for athletic clothing company** and up popped three options. Double-click on the template of your choosing and you will be guided through a series of choices.

Figure 11.1: *Certain keywords trigger Elance job posting template options.*

BEST PRACTICES

Don't sugarcoat difficult or complex aspects to your job. This will lead to unfair expectations and subpar results. It's better to find those contractors that are up to the task than it is to work through rats' nests later on.

In Figure 11.2, you are offered choices for what type of logo you want designed. In place of the project description, you are asked to briefly describe your business. Fill this out so the contractor understands your company's purpose, and click on which logo style appeals to you.

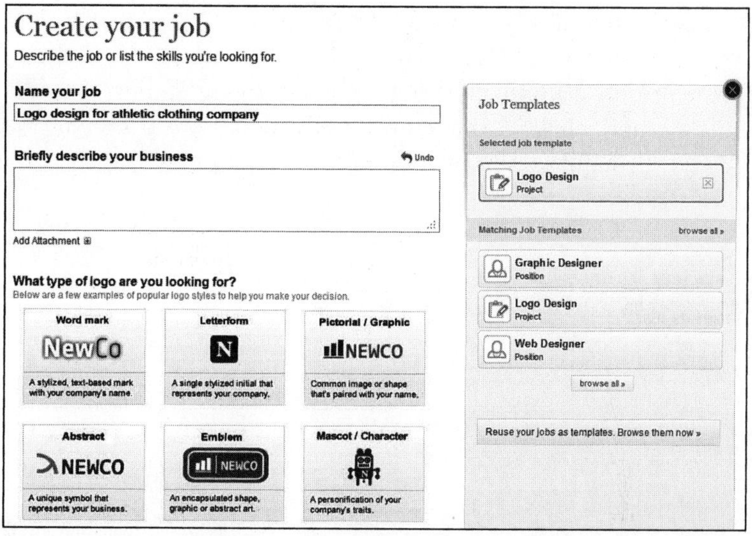

Figure 11.2: *Elance walks you through the process of tailoring your job posting.*

After the logo specifics are chosen, you will be directed to choose colors and style before you go to the normal posting parameters like price range, specific skills, etc. For generic jobs, this can greatly streamline the process and provide quality results.

The template may not serve your needs specifically, so you'll need to go in and rewrite aspects. Elance allows for this. Simply highlight and delete what doesn't apply, and then write in what does.

In Figure 11.3, maybe the template job posting description doesn't match your job requirements exactly. However, the template does provide a structure for you to work within. It's a matter of going in and rewriting the material to suit your job.

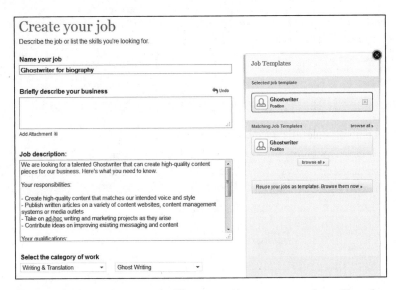

Figure 11.3: *In this example, Elance provides a structure that will need to be adjusted.*

The Contractors' View

When posting your jobs and in your attempt to attract the best talent possible, it's important to understand what the contractors themselves are looking for. How do they see the world of job postings? When you know this, you know how to speak to them on their own terms.

Top contractors consistently look for the following:

- Clearly describe projects so they can make a realistic bid.

- Don't play games with contractors or try to manipulate them into lower prices.

- A friendly and positive attitude means you might be pleasant to work for.

- Offer a realistic budget and timeline. Contractors know that if you're not realistic here, you won't be in other aspects of the job either.

- Don't speak down to contractors. They're professionals.

All in all, it's pretty straightforward. If you follow the advice in this chapter, you'll be well on your way to crafting effective job postings so you can attract the best freelancer talent the globe has to offer.

A Productive Posting Structure

Creating a skeletal structure for your job postings will allow you to go back to them time and again. They will vary according to the depth and complexity of the job, the work itself, how many people are involved, etc. But you can isolate key sections within which you fill the details.

Summary

Begin with the end in mind. This description is a summary of what you want and who you are. It doesn't need to be long; it can take just a sentence or two. But it gives contractors a general idea of what's expected.

BEST PRACTICES

In presenting your job to potential contractors, the Golden Rule is a useful guide. If you were in their shoes, how would you want to be treated? Use this as your guideline and you'll do just fine.

If you're looking for a lead generating strategy, are you a "business that wants to increase your sales volume"? Or are you an "ecommerce business specializing in marketing garden supplies to organic vegetable growers"? The second description pinpoints the situation in a much clearer way.

Details

Next come the project details. You've done your homework by now and know what you want, so now's the point where you list them. You have two angles to work with.

First, what specific qualities and parameters do you want accomplished? This includes technology, word counts, deadlines, milestones, etc. Really, it's the meat of your project.

Next, consider what specific skills you would like your contractor to have. Is she an expert on PHP? Or has she done administrative work previously for a fast-growing start-up? Maybe you want someone who's already been published to ghostwrite your grandaddy's memoirs.

Whichever it is, now is your chance to lay it all out there. Bullet points work great for this. State what you want, what skills you'd like them to have, when you want it done by, and in what form you want it done. Be sure to clearly outline the milestones and deadlines.

Questions and Why You?

Next, ask your questions. Get them to explain why they should be the one to take on your project. Good contractors will jump all over this. If you have presented yourself as a professional and fair client, they will want to work for you. If they want to work for you, they will answer your questions and often come back at you with more.

It's this beginning dance that so often isolates who the real contenders for the position will be. By asking questions, you're putting it out into the cyber universe that you're ready to communicate and get the ball rolling. Chances are you'll be pleased with the results.

Streamline

The final step is to make sure your posting is concise and streamlined. You don't want to go rambling on for ages about the intricacies of your project. The key is to deliver the facts, and just the facts, in a pleasant and upbeat way. Review your posting and make sure it's tight and fluff-less. Contractors don't want to have to struggle to get your message.

The Least You Need to Know

- The key is to describe your project needs as clearly as possible.

- Title your job carefully.

- Asking questions of contractors helps you see which contractors are most responsive and establishes rapport early on.

- For standard or repeat job postings, use Elance job post templates.

- Remember that your actions and professionalism are being judged by the contractors, too.

- Use the basic posting structure provided to make sure you cover every issue.

Selecting the Right Contractor

In This Chapter

- Similarities versus differences in hiring online and in person
- Organizing and rating the inflow of proposals
- Key factors in assessing proposals
- Actions you can take to further your selection process
- Hiring more than one contractor to test-drive their services
- The mechanics of selecting your hire(s)

Evaluating the contractors who bid on your project is a critical part of the entire online work world equation. Just like in traditional hiring, you can make good and bad decisions regarding picking the right person. In fact, you might think the problem is worse online as you don't have the normal ability of meeting face-to-face.

However, you do have a surprising number of tools at your disposal that aren't commonly thought of or used in traditional hiring. I will go through these tools and other advantages that hiring online provides. And I will take you through the process of sorting amongst the virtual stacks of job proposals submitted by contractors to find the gems that lie within.

Part of the challenge is simply adjusting to the new view you will have of your prospective hires. This isn't good or bad, it just is. Businesses worldwide are increasing their freelancing and online hires. If they can make it work, there's no reason you shouldn't be able to as well. Let's get started!

Hiring Online vs. In Person

You might think that hiring online is a bit like being asked to pick someone for a date while being blindfolded and gagged. I mean, you can't see them or talk to them in person. How on earth can you trust them with your project and end up even having to pay them?

Many clients say the advantages of hiring online actually outweigh the disadvantages. As you'll see, you do have many advantages online that your brick-and-mortar associates don't. One of the best features is you have instant access to talent from across the globe, not just your own town or city.

Remember, many of the qualities you're looking for online are the same as those in person. They will simply appear differently. You want someone who acts professionally, is on time, speaks clearly and thoughtfully, and has the background and credentials to show they've done something at least similar to what you're asking.

All these aspects can be "seen" online, too. So take your hiring know-how, and use it online. You don't have to reinvent the wheel. The biggest difference is you probably won't meet face-to-face. But looks can deceive and actions speak.

Determine Your Hiring Criteria

Clients with the most success at hiring online know the criteria they're looking for in contractors before they begin. If you haven't done this already, stop and do it now. Think about what the most important criteria are to you.

These factors could be experience, speed of response to questions, positive feedback, portfolio samples, creativity in finding solutions or new angles, price, time to complete the project, location, or myriad other factors. Write them down and use these to assess your potential hires. The clearer you are in what you want, the more easily you'll come to the right conclusion.

It's a Tsunami!

Depending on your project, you may start receiving proposals within minutes of clicking on the Post Job button. Remember, your project will be available around the globe. Contractors are searching for work 24/7.

When I had a website made, I received my first proposal within two minutes of posting, and at the end of 24 hours I had more than 30 sitting in my inbox. This is common, but not all postings receive this type of attention. If you're looking for organic rodent recipes to feed your pet boa constrictor, you may experience only a few responses, but rarely will you get skunked completely. Experts exist for everything, and you can find them online.

 BEST PRACTICES

Many clients start sorting through their proposals as soon as they receive them and make initial assessments. More time will be spent later reviewing the contractors in detail, but splitting them into A, B, and C files right off the bat helps keep the process under control.

As the proposals pile in, it will take time to give each of them the attention they deserve. Allow for this. You may receive dozens of proposals, and for most of us, making good hires takes time. It's important to give each applicant his or her due and see which ones stand out from the rest.

The Proposal Page

Elance has a workroom specifically designed to manage the proposals received for your job. You will refer to this page often as you sort through the contractors. To get to it, click on the little house in the far-left corner of the main toolbar. This home button always takes you to your My Jobs page listing your projects. Then click on the heading of the project you want to view the proposals on.

I'll go through each of the key workroom areas.

Overview

At the top of the page you'll see a basic overview of what project you posted, what your actual posting said, and how many contractors have bid. This layout will appear each time you open this page.

In the box on the right, tabs run along the top. The first says Overview and is what you see in Figure 12.1. You get the summary of what's going on overall, and can see who you invited and how many of them responded.

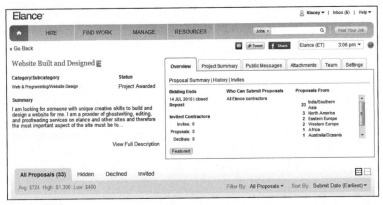

Figure 12.1: *The Overview area of the workroom gives you a clear snapshot of the project and who's bidding.*

The Project Summary tab brings up your project description. This is a handy way to remind yourself what exactly you said and asked for. Can't remember all the details you listed for your website? You've got it all here.

In the Public Messages tab, you can add a message to your job posting that will also be sent directly to all contractors who've placed a bid. This is a great way to clarify specs or terms, or answer any questions that are consistently popping up.

The Attachments tab is where you upload an attachment. Maybe you have more project details or sample work that would more clearly explain what you're looking for. Remember, communication is key. Don't be shy about using these extra ways to be clear about your project.

After you add an attachment it will be updated on the job post, but be sure to post a public message as well to let contractors know. They won't be notified that an attachment has been added otherwise.

Under Team, you can view everyone involved on the client side of the project. All your team members as well as their roles will be listed here.

Finally, the Settings tab lets you adjust your bidding and payment parameters. For example, this is where you would go if you wanted to cancel a project or extend or end the bidding time. You can also adjust basic payment settings.

The Proposals

Each bid you receive on your job will include the actual proposal the contractor writes, plus myriad extra details that appear in the workroom, as shown in Figure 12.2.

Figure 12.2: *Each bid you receive will arrive in the form of a summary and will be listed in the workroom.*

The proposal itself is displayed on the left side of the box. With the click of a mouse, it can be expanded to full view.

BEST PRACTICES

Given the quantity of contractor bids coming in, it's best to use the note-taking feature early and often. Don't rely solely on your memory or on that little sticky note clinging precariously to your monitor. The more regularly you write down relevant details, questions, and concerns, the easier it will be to find your answers and select the right contractor.

On the top you have the basic summary of this contractor's statistics. You know where they're located, how many jobs they've had over the course of the last 12 months, and what their average rating is. There's also a direct link to their portfolio samples and their profile.

On the right side you're able to message them directly and privately. This is enormously useful in the selection process. There's also an area for making your own notes, which the contractor cannot see. This is great for listing questions or concerns you want to follow up on.

The bottom-right corner is where you can take specific action. You can hide the bid, which is useful if you've decided against them and don't want to scroll past every time. If you decline their bid they will be notified directly, as they will if you click the green **Select** button and choose them for the job.

One of the clever features of the proposal summary box is the ability you have to sort and rate your contractors. On the top-right corner you have a rating system from 1 to 5. Use this early!

Many clients make a first assessment of the proposals and right off give them a 1, 3, or 5 green-dot rating. This helps them make an initial sort. Later, they can go through each one more carefully.

Two additional avenues exist to sort your proposals, as shown in Figure 12.3. On the top-right corner, two drop-down menus (Filter By and Sort By) are available. Now you can manage your prospective contractors by sorting for feedback, bid amount, your own ratings, and more. This is a super-convenient way to stay on top of things.

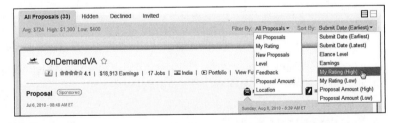

Figure 12.3: *These two drop-down menus give you several interesting ways to sort through your proposals.*

Assessing the Proposals

Next comes reviewing and managing the actual proposals. This is one of the most critical steps. After your initial impression and rating, take a closer look at each proposal and revise your first opinion if appropriate.

> **BEST PRACTICES**
>
> One top client, Ken Lancaster, who's posted over 400 projects on Elance, uses these three criteria for hiring successfully. One: High feedback ratings, 4.9 to 5 as averages. Two: Hire those freelancers that do this for a living, not as a side job. You can tell by the quantity of projects they do. Three: Look for high-quality work samples of the same type of work as you're looking for.

Make a list of the most important qualities you're looking for and see which contractors exhibited these. Much information can be gained from the proposal, so read each one carefully. This isn't the only feature you'll use to make your assessment, but it's an important one.

Did They Listen?

Unfortunately, the cut-and-paste proposal beast is alive and well in the online work world. You will recognize these proposals immediately because they have nothing, or almost nothing, describing your distinct requests. Fortunately, you can spot these easily. Many top clients throw out all boilerplate proposals without a second glance.

Have a look at the following. This came in response to a detailed request for building a website:

> "At the outset, thanks for taking the time to review our bid for this project. Take one look at our portfolio site and you'll know why we should be 'the' choice for this assignment.
>
> At our firm, we build brands, visual identities, and interactive web solutions that distinguish our clients from the crowd. With hundreds of clients in 21 countries, and over 12 years in the trenches—we've learned the art of keeping good company and staying ahead.
>
> We are passionate about what we do, and would like to hear from you on how we can serve your needs. Come on in."

Sounds good? But there's not one detail that shows they read the project posting or assimilated and understood what was requested. This same response would work for thousands of jobs. Beware of this.

Questions Answered?

As you know from Chapter 11, one way to assess a contractor's quality is to ask questions in your job posting. You can do this as a test to see if they respond, as many clients do, but also to genuinely see what they suggest for solving the issue at hand. If they don't answer your questions, they aren't paying attention.

Do They Understand?

Does the contractor have a clear grasp of what the job entails? If you want a series of articles written, does she understand the timeline, copy length, scope of material, and voice you're asking for? Top contractors will let you know they understand in their proposals.

> **CYBER SNAGS**
>
> A red flag should go up when a contractor only wants to discuss the details of the project by phone or skype, not through workroom messaging. You don't want to be in a position where they can say anything they want to close the deal, but you have no way to follow up and prove what they said. At the outset, communicate in such a way that you have a written record, preferably on Elance.

When a contractor asks you a question about the job, it's a good sign. If they want something clarified, it means they're listening. Watch for these and give them extra points.

Tally Up

When you've finished assessing the proposals, you will have a much clearer idea of who's a serious candidate for your job. You will have eliminated a large percentage of the overall bidders. Take this smaller group of potential contractors and get to know them even better with these next steps.

Reviewing Profiles

At the top of the same profile summary box, you have an easy link directly to the contractor's profile. Go here next. Or you can simply click on the contractor's name. You learned a lot about profiles in Chapter 10, so you've already got the basics down. Now it's time to apply what you know to your end decision of who to hire.

Go down your list of hiring criteria and see where each contractor lands. A few points to consider are:

- Look at feedback. Read what previous clients have said, and specifically, read the negative or less than perfect comments. A busy contractor will be bound to have had a bad work experience; it happens to the best of us. But look for any consistencies in the negative comments. Are they consistently late? Is the quality questioned each time?

- Do they commonly do the same type of job as yours? If they do, it's a good sign.

- Check out their portfolio. A popular contractor may do great work at a reasonable price, but if their style isn't what you're looking for, the match still won't work. Make sure you like their look, feel, sound, or writing style, whatever applies.

- Price is *not* king. "You get what you pay for" can easily be applied to online work. Yes, great bargains are to be had. But if the work isn't what you wanted, it was money wasted all the same. Price should be one factor, but not the only factor.

- Check out the new contractors. It may take a little more due diligence, but give these guys a chance. Every star was new once.

- Consider how many repeat clients they have. This can be a positive sign.

- Consider if their credentials are verified or not. This isn't a deal breaker, but is a sign in their favor.

Get Proactive

You should be assessing each contractor from the very first contact. Do they answer your questions quickly and thoroughly? Do they seem to have a firm grasp on what you're looking for? Beware that the courtship might be better than the marriage, but at least you'll get an idea of what their work habits are.

CYBER SNAGS

Don't forget to take into account the different time zones and holidays when communicating with prospective contractors. An eight-hour delay in response may just mean it's the middle of the night for them. And they may have different religious or cultural holidays that temporarily interrupt the workflow.

You also need to be responsive to their questions. Set the example that you're professional, legitimate, and a great client to work for. This will help the best contractors choose to work for you. It's a two-way street, don't forget.

Jeff Crystal, COO at Voltaic Systems (www.voltaicsystems.com), has used Elance hires extensively to build his business. Selecting the right contractor is critical in his eyes. Jeff says, "For us, it isn't so much the money lost [if you hire the wrong person], but the time spent trying to manage someone who isn't quite right."

In this light, being proactive in assessing who's best is a great way to speed up the selection process. What you actually choose to do will depend on your project, but consider the following ideas.

Key Questions

Sometimes a well-placed question will reveal a potential problem. The issue may be big enough that you choose not to work with that contractor, or they may be perfectly manageable once you know they exist.

Consider the following three questions successful Elance clients use with prospective hires:

- Tell me about a job that went bad. This might lead to revealing how they solve problems or what type of relationship skills they have.

- Is there anything that could keep you from completing this project on time? Find potential bugaboos in the form of vacations or different cultural or religious holidays.

- Is there anything you think I'm missing in this project before I get started? This opens up how creative or keyed into your vision they are. If they give you a canned response to sell more services, that's one thing. But they also might genuinely identify gaps you hadn't thought of.

Test-Drives

One of the most common bits of advice successful clients have regarding how to hire contractors is to give them a small project to do first. Sometimes due to the nature of the project this isn't practical. But often it's the key to seeing how they really function.

CYBER SNAGS

It's absolutely forbidden by Elance to ask a contractor to do work for free. You can't ask them to do sample writing, but you can ask them for samples of writing. You can't request trial programming, but you can ask to see what they've done in the past.

One way to do this is to break your project into chunks and give a piece to a few different contractors. This way the job still gets done, but you see how each contractor works for consideration when the bigger projects begin.

Another way is to have a select few contractors do the same job for you. At the beginning this is more expensive, but it can pay off big in the long run. Now you'll really know who does the job the best, on time, and in a positive and creative way.

The Phone Interview

Many clients swear by the phone or Skype interview. This is done only for short-listed prospects and gives you the chance to see how they respond to your questions. Know what you're going to ask in advance, and try to think of nonstandard questions to get them thinking outside the box.

Through these conversations, you can get into the nitty-gritty of the project. You also become one step closer to them because you're having real interaction. Be sure to take notes and confirm anything you agree on in an email afterward.

Diamonds in the Rough

I've said it before and I'll say it again, don't overlook the new folks. You may need to dig a little deeper, but the key is new contractors need you as much as you need them. They're on Elance because they want to grow their freelancing business. Good feedback and ratings are key to this and many will tell you that right up front.

> **BEST PRACTICES**
>
> A great way to filter new contractors is to simply outright ask them, "Why should I hire you over these other, more experienced contractors?" They will then tell you in detail the advantages they bring to the table. Try it, you might just be impressed.

New contractors have the incentive to work harder and to make sure you're happy. Obviously, not all will succeed in their freelancing careers, and some may just be testing the online waters. This is where your hiring selection process, as discussed previously, comes into play. But don't automatically delete someone from your proposal list because they're new. Look for those diamonds in the rough.

The Bottom Line

By now you've compiled data on each contractor and you probably have a short list at the ready. Clients comment over and over again how most of the time the bottom line isn't about the price. When you see the talent that comes through your inbox, you'll realize that most of the time the lowest price doesn't mean the best deal.

Overall, Elance can save clients enormous amounts of money. But this has a lot to do with the advantageous logistics of working online. Shop around, but don't get locked into a restrictive cost-is-most-important mindset. You're doing yourself a disservice if you do.

Closing the Deal

So you've made your short list, asked your questions, and assessed the feedback received. You've made your choice as to who you want to hire and you're anxious to get going. Now what?

BEST PRACTICES

Unless the project is too small, it's wisest to request milestones from your contractor. This gives both parties a time and payment schedule to work from.

Easy. In the bottom-right corner of the proposal summary box of the contractor you've chosen, click the big green **Select** button, as shown in Figure 12.4, and you're on your way. You'll be led through the simple process of completing your hire.

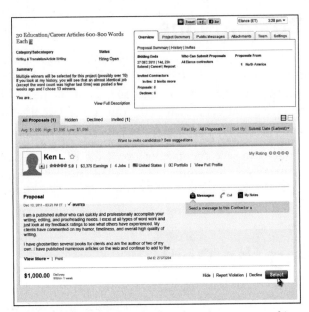

Figure 12.4: *Use the **Select** button on the proposal summary to hire a contractor.*

If you want to hire more than one contractor, simply do the same process all over again. Click **Select** for each contractor you want to hire for the project.

Both you and the contractor will be asked to confirm the terms and milestones. Once you both agree, click **Submit** (see Figure 12.5) and the project will be live.

Once you've both agreed to the conditions of the job, you can begin to work together. The terms and milestones can be changed, but again, both parties must agree. The system makes this all quite fluid and intuitive.

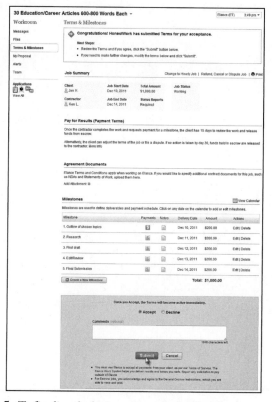

Figure 12.5: *To finalize the hiring process, both sides must agree to the terms and milestones.*

The Least You Need to Know

- Select your main hiring criteria before you begin reviewing proposals.
- Sort and rank your prospects as you go along.
- Post new public messages to update any information on your job post that will help prospective hires.
- Assessing proposals includes seeing if they listened to you as an individual, if they answered your questions, and if they have a firm grasp on what you want from the project.
- Proactively ask your short list candidates key questions and interview them over the phone or Skype.
- New contractors can be great prospective hires, but you may need to dig a little deeper in the question-and-answer process.

Managing Your Projects

Chapter

13

In This Chapter

- The ins and outs of the client workroom
- Features for building teams
- Managing hourly jobs
- Utilizing awesome applications in your virtual office
- Nurturing the client-contractor relationship

In an ideal online work world, you will develop go-to contractors that you either employ all the time, or rehire each time you have new projects to complete. Many long-term work relationships are created and maintained in the Elance environment. Naturally, it's easier to work with someone you're comfortable and familiar with than it is to go out searching for a new contractor each time you have a project.

A critical part of developing this type of relationship takes place during the job itself. Managing your projects partly entails using the right tools and gadgets Elance provides. But the other part, and one too often left to the side, is managing the human relationship. Contractors and clients alike want to be respected and valued.

By looking after the people who are taking the time and effort to do your job in the best way possible, you'll be fostering excellence and ongoing symbiotic relationships. Oftentimes, this will happen between people on opposite ends of the globe.

Navigating the Elance Workroom

After you award the project, set the milestones, and both parties have agreed to everything, you will then use the workroom for day-to-day managing of your project. You access this workroom by clicking on the house in the top-left corner of the main toolbar. This will bring up a list of all your jobs. Click on the title of the one you want to view.

Whether for a client or contractor, the project workroom looks the same. It opens up to the message board where you can post messages, as you can see in Figure 13.1. The messages are also forwarded by email to the contractor. On the left side is a menu of resources, many of which I'll go through in this chapter.

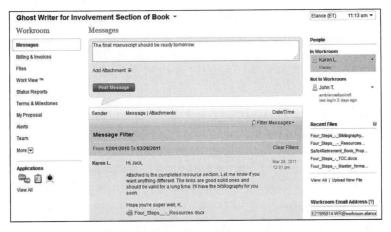

Figure 13.1: *The client workroom is where you will manage the day-to-day activities of the job.*

From the message board you can also upload attachments, and on the right side you can see those that have been uploaded by you or your contractor. You can see if the contractor is online and invite them to a meeting.

The workroom is also where you can access various *applications* to smooth the workflow process. I get into these later in this chapter.

DEFINITION

Applications are technical tools specifically designed to help make your virtual office as user-friendly as possible. They include Elance's Work View, video conferencing, screen sharing, and a format for managing code in a collaborative setting.

Prefunding Milestones

As I mentioned in the last chapter, I highly recommend that you use milestones in your project setup. This gives both you and your contractor a clear structure to work by. Milestones apply to fixed-price projects, not hourly ones.

You also have the option for *prefunding milestones*. This is where you place funds in escrow at Elance, before they're due. The contractor will not have access to the money until you release it from escrow. If you cancel the project or change the agreed-upon terms, the money will be refunded back to you. In other words, it's safe there.

DEFINITION

Prefunding milestones refers to placing funds in escrow before they are due to be paid. This is often done by clients at the beginning of a project.

The advantage to prefunding milestones is the action clearly shows the contractor you're serious about paying them for the work they're doing. In their eyes, this is a sign of a good client. After all, much of the time they're doing at least part of the work before they get paid.

To prefund the milestones you can click on **Payments** on the menu on the left. Or you can click on **Manage** on the top toolbar. Then click on **Payments** from the drop-down menu. Both avenues lead to the same end.

File Sharing and Status Reports

These are two tools you'll use frequently as a client. Both are accessed from the menu on the left of the workroom. Using the file sharing system allows you to easily monitor and assess the work being done. It also means you have an automatic record of everything shared.

Status reports are required on all fixed-price jobs (while timesheets are required on hourly jobs). The contractor is required to post a status report every week before midnight on Sunday. You will receive notification of this as well as if there's a problem or any action that needs to be taken.

Teams

As with contractors, clients can also form teams (see Figure 13.2). For larger projects this is an enormous help. Maybe you're busy with your start-up company and need to get the work done but don't have time to manage the project yourself. In this case you can still keep tabs on what's going on, but your team member will handle the day-to-day management of the project.

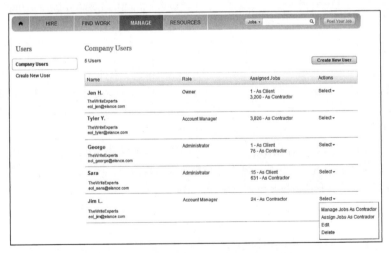

Figure 13.2: *Client teams are managed here.*

In client accounts, these roles are available:

- **Owner.** This person has access to all account functions, including the payment and withdrawal of funds.

- **Administrator.** Also has access to all functions.

- **Hiring Manager.** Can handle all functions of specific projects assigned to them by the administrator.

- **Staff.** The worker bee. This person can view status reports, timesheets, proposals, and can communicate via workroom messaging. A staff member cannot handle money, deal with contracts, or change terms or milestones.

Tracker and Work View

Tracker and *Work View* are both tools to help with managing hourly jobs.

> **DEFINITION**
>
> **Tracker** and **Work View** work together and are optional on hourly projects. Tracker tracks the amount of time a contractor spends on a specific project. Work View takes random and sporadic snapshots of the contractor's computer screen and delivers them to the client. Both parties must agree to the use of these two tools before they can be implemented.

Tracker (see Figure 13.3) is a tool the contractor can download, which when switched on logs the time the contractor is spending on her computer. It then sends this data into a timesheet for the client. The client is given a weekly tally of the time spent and, unless he disputes the charges, the contractor is automatically paid five days later. The timesheet is delivered to the client before midnight on Sunday.

Work View is a function that works in conjunction with Tracker and again is optional. With Tracker on, the contractor can also enable Work View, which will take regular screenshots throughout each hour the contractor is logged in as working. The images are viewable from the Work View page inside the project workroom.

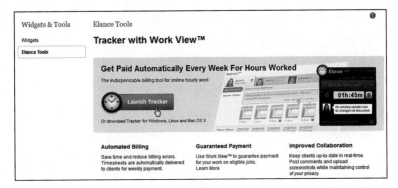

Figure 13.3: *Tracker and Work View are designed to help clients manage hourly jobs.*

The client can now review the images of the contractor's screen and verify they were working on their project rather than hanging out on Facebook. If the client doesn't dispute the time recorded in the timesheet within five days, the contractor gets paid automatically the following Friday.

The quality of the work is not guaranteed. So if the client is unhappy with the design logo, he can't dispute the bill over this. He can only dispute the amount of time spent. If Work View is used and the screenshots show his project being worked on, then he can't dispute the time.

Pros and Cons

The advantages to Tracker and Work View are:

- The client has a way to track hourly jobs. If she wants, she can also actually see the work being done that she's paying for.

- The computerized timesheets and automatic payments save time for clients.

- The contractor knows that if she spends the amount of time she says she does on the project, she'll be guaranteed her weekly payment.

- For contractors, this reduces billing errors or delayed payments. If there's no contest to the timesheet, the money goes directly and automatically to the contractor's account.

BEST PRACTICES

Some top-notch contractors refuse to use Tracker and Work View. Whatever their reason, remember to allow for their concerns and opinions. If you pass them by because they say no to your request to use these tools, you might be missing out on great work done. First, listen to their reasoning, then make your decision.

The disadvantages to Tracker and Work View are:

- The contractor can feel mistrusted to do the job he said he would. Some feel it's equivalent to Big Brother.

- Contractors have different work styles, some of which include excelling at multitasking. To work solely on one project is unnatural and counterproductive for them.

If the contractor forgets to turn on Tracker and Work View, he can email the client and explain what happened. But it's up to the client to believe him and instigate a payment manually.

Using Tracker and Work View

Tracker and Work View are quite easy to use. Review the Tracker time logs to see the number of hours worked and when. To view the Work View screenshots, simply click on **Work View** in the left-hand menu of the project workroom. Here you will see the random screenshots taken of the contractor's work, as in Figure 13.4.

You can easily manage individuals or teams from the Work View interface and see your projects unfold right before your eyes.

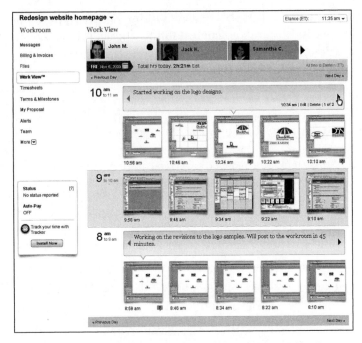

Figure 13.4: *As an optional feature, Work View can be used to take screenshots of what the contractor is working on.*

Wondrous Widgets

Elance has yet more handy applications they've developed for smoothing the workflow. The neat thing is Elance keeps coming up with more and more ideas to make your online office productive and easy to use.

BEST PRACTICES

Elance is constantly upgrading their website and creating more tools and applications. Many ways exist to stay up-to-date, including visiting the blog and reading the monthly newsletter emailed to all clients and contractors. You can also visit the Apps page to see if you missed any new technological goodies.

To find these applications, go back to the project workroom. On the bottom of the left menu where it says Application, click on **View All** as you did to find Tracker. You can also access them by clicking on

Resources on the top toolbar, then clicking on **My Apps**. Once you have uploaded an application, you will be able to find it on the My Apps page. To start with, they can all be found on the All Apps page, as shown in Figure 13.5.

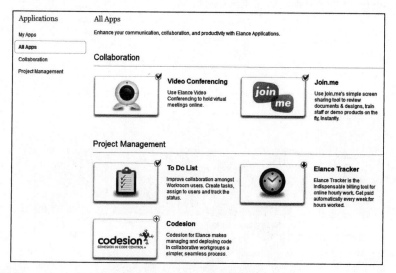

Figure 13.5: *The All Apps page has a boatload of goodies for your virtual office.*

Screen Sharing

The screen sharing feature is accessed through the orange and green Join Me icon on the All Apps page. Screen sharing is a great tool for collaborating with your contractor. Sometimes it's just plain easier to see something than it is to describe it or exchange countless emails.

CYBER SNAGS

With the Join Me screen sharing feature, if you're viewing your screen make sure you close any non-work-related applications. Share only what you want to share!

You can either set it up so your screen is the one viewed, or so that the contractor's is. You can also invite team members to join the session.

Video Conferencing

The video conferencing application (see Figure 13.6) provides an efficient way to conduct meetings with team members and contractors. Your entire team, including contractors, can now meet at once in the equivalent of a virtual conference room.

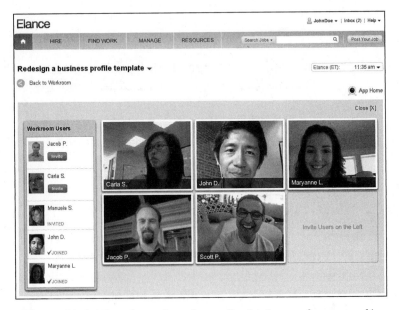

Figure 13.6: *The video conferencing application is great for team and/or contractor meetings.*

The advantages of being able to see each other are twofold. First, you can consolidate in one meeting various project details that might have taken an ocean of emails or live chats to resolve. Second, you also have a chance to meet the people you're working with and strengthen the relationship. Long-term work relationships are best for everyone involved. Video conferencing is one more way to facilitate this process.

To-Do Lists

As basic as this sounds, having a shared to-do list is a pretty practical tool. I mean, how else can you share all those yellow sticky notes decorating your computer like an otherworldly cyber-sunflower?

Take the key project points you need to do and type them in. Have your other team members or your contractors do the same. Each note is credited with who wrote it, and you can easily check them off when complete. You can also assign duties to others.

This simple little application helps coordinate the day-to-day workflow, and is one more neat feature in your virtual office.

Code Sharing

Codesion is an independent company that Elance has partnered with to facilitate *code sharing* within collaborative groups. This way each member can see and share code within the entire project. Integration with management tools like Basecamp, Rally, Atlassian JIRA and VersionOne, and FTP will actually deploy software to your live system.

DEFINITION

Code sharing describes a way two or more programmers can share the source code they are developing within the same or related projects.

You can begin with a free 30-day trial, and Elance ensures that Codesion has secure and reliable repository hosting. If code sharing is your issue, give this a try.

The Contractor-Client Relationship

In this virtual world of email, chat, and file and code sharing, it's sometimes easy to forget there's a human on the other side. Real people from all over the globe are pooling their resources to get work done.

What's critical within this environment is to not lose the personal element. If you want to nurture long-term, reliable business arrangements with great talent, you must connect with the human side. You must make the effort to understand who your contractors are and to treat them with respect and dignity.

In this age of call centers and phone menus, what people miss the most is finding a person they can connect to. This is your job as a great client: Connect with your contractor and show them you value their talent. Then, watch them shine for you. Again, it's basic human nature.

Use Your Virtual Office

The workroom features and applications I've been discussing throughout this book are there for one reason, to make the clients' and contractors' work experiences flow smoothly and easily through Elance.

Think of it from Elance's eyes. The more positive your work experience on their site, the more business you'll do there. The more business you do with Elance, the more success they'll have. Everyone's incentives are aligned, as they should be.

Given this, use those workroom features and applications because they really do help. They've been designed with just that in mind. Not all of the tools will be applicable for each project, but use those that fit. You will have a closer and better experience with your contractor(s). Many Elance clients have multi-year work relationships with their Elance contractors, and using these virtual office resources has helped.

How Much to Manage

The answer to how much to manage will vary with each client and each contractor. There is no one-size-fits-all solution. But a few guidelines from top clients and contractors alike can be implemented.

- Communicate frequently. This doesn't mean hover over their virtual shoulders and comment on each comma. It means stay in touch.

- Don't micromanage. Most freelancers hate it.

- Work within expectations. These should have been clearly outlined in the beginning (see Chapter 11).

- Don't change the job parameters without involving the contractor. This is a virtual way to pull the rug out from under your contractor's feet. If something needs to be changed, explain why and make sure it still fits within the original job description. If not, you may need to make milestone and/or payment changes.

- Prefund your milestones if it's a fixed-price job. This is a sign you're serious and contractors love it.

- Be fair. 'Nuff said.

- Be patient. If there are delays or misunderstandings, understand the other side's situation, not just your own.

- Pay on time. A sign of respect as well as professionalism.

- Give great feedback. Contractors live and die by feedback. If they've done a great job, let them know—publicly.

- Invite them to new jobs.

> **BEST PRACTICES**
>
> Many of the best clients ask up front how much their contractor wants to be managed. This is a way of getting the subject right out front and center.

Fostering Loyalty and Excellence

If you use the previous suggestions and treat your contractors well, you will be fostering loyalty and excellence. To a high degree, how people treat you is a mirror of how you treat them. Take the high road and most will join you.

There will always be those contractors you just don't click with or who don't meet your expectations. Finish the job (unless you've run into trouble; see Chapter 17), and don't hire them back. It couldn't be simpler.

One of the deep advantages of the online work world is when the job is done, it's done. You don't have to work with HR on terminating or repositioning the employee. And unemployment insurance and the like are simply irrelevant. This is fair to all involved. From the contractor's perspective, not all clients are people they'd want an ongoing relationship with either.

The key is to set up the project and expectations clearly from the beginning, communicate frequently throughout the job, and reward excellence at the end through feedback, referrals, and new job invitations.

The Least You Need to Know

- The Elance workroom is easy and intuitive.
- Tracker and Work View are optional methods to manage hourly jobs.
- Screen sharing and video conferencing are great ways to communicate with your team and contractor(s).
- Codesion is a handy code sharing application.
- With respect and communication, long-term work relationships are possible.

Advanced Elancing for Contractors and Clients

This part covers some of the more detailed areas of the Elance virtual work platform for both contractors and clients. Elance doesn't just serve to introduce contractors and clients, but also provides a safe and effective work environment. Project agreements, Terms of Service, and contractor and client online safety is reviewed.

I provide a detailed description of how money flows securely through Elance, and give in-depth instructions on how to fine-tune account settings. Many contractors and clients alike don't realize the full list of opportunities at the end of jobs, including repeat business and referrals. I discuss these as well as include a troubleshooting guide for what to do if you end up with an unproductive business relationship. It doesn't happen often, but it's best to know what to do if it does.

This part finishes with a chapter on the Elance community. Advice, help, and camaraderie exist amongst Elancers, and I'll show you how to get involved.

The Nuts and Bolts of the Deal

In This Chapter

- How Elance protects clients' and contractors' work experiences
- Using templates to establish legal agreements
- Additional tax compliance and insurance solutions
- Basic Elance rules and regulations
- Tailoring your privacy settings

Without a clear and fair structure, Elance and the online work world cannot exist. The benefits of a global source of freelancers and jobs would be outweighed by the risks involved. Fortunately, many structures and tools are available to ensure a smooth and stable work environment.

From legal agreement templates, to enhanced privacy settings, to administrative business solutions, Elance has built a platform that enables hundreds of thousands of dollars every day to be exchanged. In this chapter, you will learn about the nuts and bolts of the Elance world that keep the foundation in place.

Protecting Both Sides

In the third quarter of 2011, over 150,000 jobs were posted on Elance. This amounts to over 50,000 new jobs per month and almost 1,700 a day. With the growth Elance has seen since inception, and an over 100 percent increase in the last year alone, you can expect that the number of jobs posted will continue to rise.

In the same vein, and closer to the hearts and wallets of clients and contractors alike, over $37 million passed from clients to contractors in the same quarter. This means over $12.5 million per month and over a whopping $400,000 in transactions per day. Elance is big business and expanding fast.

All this is good news for clients and contractors alike. More and more work is available while simultaneously the quantity of freelancing talent to choose from increases by the thousands each week. It also underlines the changing business-scape of the world.

With all this ecommerce going on and money changing hands, how is Elance protecting both sides of the equation? This is an important question and one worth spending time exploring. We can look at it from a couple of perspectives.

One, how is Elance ensuring the smooth communication and agreement of business terms through its platform? It's one step to agree on a project, and another to outline the legal terms and conditions and ensure the smooth flow of payments.

Two, how is this accomplished all the while walking the fine line between sharing information yet maintaining privacy?

> **CYBER SNAGS**
>
> Elance provides legal agreements for the use of clients and contractors. However, the cleanest way to solve trouble is to avoid it in the first place. Establish a habit of always communicating clearly, nip problems in the bud before they grow into oaks, and use these contracts to set a professional tone.

Project Agreements

Project agreements are available and entered into within the Elance system. Each is designed to make sure the transactions are secure from a legal perspective. Elance provides samples that you can tailor to your specific needs. These are a great resource for both sides of the deal.

To locate the templates Elance provides, go to the **Help** menu in the upper-right corner of the My Jobs page. Type in **sample agreements** in the search box, as shown in Figure 14.1. This will take you to the Word document entitled "Sample Contract Agreements" (see Figure 14.2).

Figure 14.1: *Find sample project agreements through Help.*

Click on any of the links to open a particular agreement. Remember, these forms are simply templates for your use and Elance doesn't take any responsibility for them or guarantee what they say. But they do provide a starting point that is an excellent resource.

NDAs

Nondisclosure agreements are commonly used with Elance projects, as in work everywhere. The two NDA templates Elance offers (refer to Figure 14.2) give you the skeletal structure with which to move forward. They work pretty well, but if you have any questions or concerns, see your attorney.

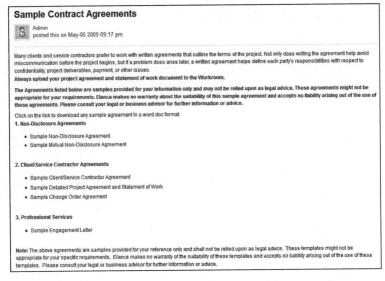

Figure 14.2: *Sample contract agreements Elance provides.*

Client/Contractor Agreements

Two versions of this are available and in both you lay out the terms and conditions of the project. One is called the Client/ Service Contractor Agreement and the other is the Detailed Project Agreement and Statement of Work. As the names imply, one is more detailed than the other.

Within each you also clearly establish the intellectual property rights, and the conditions for terminating the relationship are laid out. There is a section for adding your own clauses as well.

BEST PRACTICES

While utilizing the agreement templates isn't required, contractors and clients both like the fact they can add this layer of legal security to the project.

As you can see in Figure 14.3, you are provided with the structure and instructions as to what to fill in where. You tailor the details to your specific project and both sides must agree and sign before it takes effect. Remember, these aren't foolproof, but they're useful tools.

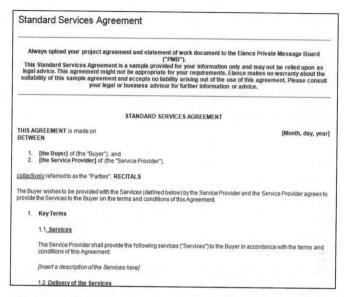

Figure 14.3: *The client/contractor service agreement template.*

Change Order Agreement and Letter of Engagement

The final two templates are what their titles state. The Change Order Agreement allows both sides to lay out in writing what the changes are, why they occurred, and the new parameters required to complete the job.

The Engagement Letter allows both sides to clarify the description of services and fees. Short and sweet.

Agreements with Elance

Certain default agreements are established when you become a member of Elance and later when you enter into your first transactions. The Terms of Service are agreed to when you open your account. You can find the nitty-gritty by clicking on the link to **Terms of Service** at the bottom of the Elance homepage.

Here you can explore the fine print and rules and regulations of Elance. Have a look around, there's lots of good information here. I'll go through some of the important information in this and other chapters.

Terms of Service

The Terms of Service can be accessed from the menu in the middle of the page. As with many legal documents, this document serves as a great cure for insomnia. However, it also lays out the full deal between all parties involved: the contractor, client, and Elance.

Service Agreements

One of two service agreements is automatically entered into with Elance when you award, or are awarded, a job. For standard transactions, it's titled the Services Agreement between Client and Contractor. For those using the Elance payroll service, the Elance Payroll Services Agreement is the default. These provide the fine print in what the two parties agree to.

Protection Online

One of the major objections to working and hiring online is what to do about safety. Folks with the best of intentions love to tell riveting stories of identity and financial theft online. Much of this is exaggerated, but as with all exaggerations, there is usually a core of truth.

Yes, sharks cruise the online waters. Some lurk quietly in the shallows, waiting for innocent consumers and business owners to wade by. Others actively target and hunt their prey. No system is entirely safe, but so far Elance has been pretty darn good. Given the quantity of jobs and funds that trade hands, the number of abuses is minute.

However, it's always best to know what actions you can take to protect yourself online. And you should understand what Elance is doing on your behalf in the same arena.

To get started, click on **Resources** in the main upper toolbar. Then click on **Trust & Safety**. On the left side will be a short menu, which I cover next.

Elance Policies

These cover the rules and regs of Elance-land. As you read through them, you will realize they are designed to protect both parties and none should surprise you.

The basics include:

- You may not offer your services for free or ask for services for free.
- You may not bid below the Elance minimums.
- You may not accept or offer payment off the Elance system.
- You may not offer payment on a commission or royalty basis.
- In your proposal you may not include any contact information away from Elance such as a phone number or Skype address.
- You may not submit sample material that isn't your own.
- You may not violate the Terms of Service or any outside law.

Pretty straightforward stuff, and there's a bit more but this covers the core. This framework helps provide the stable work environment that Elance offers.

BEST PRACTICES

It's best for both parties to keep the Elance world as clean and professional as possible. Everybody wins this way. However, Elance itself can only do so much—which is actually quite a lot. If you see someone violating a rule, report them. It makes it a better community for all of us.

Protect Your Account

This section is full of great advice on how to protect yourself online. As I've mentioned, abuses on Elance are rare, but that doesn't mean they don't happen and won't again in the future.

In a nutshell:

- Create a secure password (Elance shows you the best way) and make sure it's different from your normal email password.

- Always use your own virus and spyware software protection.

- Elance encrypts your financial information so it's safe. Therefore, never email or workroom message your personal financial information to someone, no matter how good their excuse.

- Elance will never send you an email asking you to confirm your password or financial information. If you receive any suspicious email claiming to be from them, report it immediately.

- High step away from counterfeit or money order scams. If you're ever in doubt, contact Elance directly.

- Don't let a potential client talk you into working for lower pay at the beginning with a promise of more work in the future.

- Don't respond to a job that asks you to buy something (like a user manual) in order to complete the work.

The list goes on, so check out this section of the site for details and examples. Understanding potential dangers is the first step in avoiding them.

Privacy and Elance

Obviously, the privacy and protection of your personal and financial information is paramount to any long-term successful business venture, online or otherwise. Without this trust the foundation will quickly crumble.

Given the quantity of financial transactions Elance does in any given day, week, or year, it's no surprise they've spent a lot of time working on member privacy. It wouldn't work otherwise; it's as simple as that.

> **BEST PRACTICES**
>
> Some Elancers like to keep their earnings and/or amount spent on projects private. Others use this information to prove they're active and successful. The choice is completely yours and can be changed at any time.

Your financial information is encrypted within Elance and cannot be accessed by anyone unauthorized. They use the same encryption technology that most major ecommerce sites use and will continue to update. In order to access your account information you have to use a user name and password. This is all pretty standard stuff.

Additional privacy settings can be found by clicking on your user name in the top-right corner of most any Elance page. In the drop-down menu, click on **Settings**. In the menu on the left, click on **Privacy Settings** to see the screen shown in Figure 14.4.

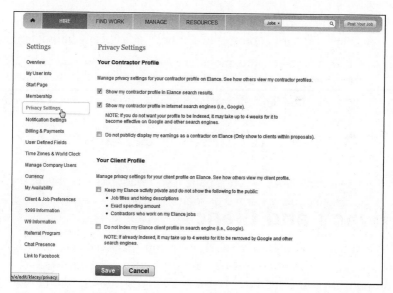

Figure 14.4: *Elance privacy settings give you the opportunity to hide your earnings, job titles, and other information.*

For contractors, you can choose to keep the amount you've earned on Elance public or private. If you select the private option, those numbers will only be available to potential clients whose projects you've bid on.

For clients, you can choose to keep the total amount you've spent on Elance private or public, as well as the job names and descriptions. There's no real right or wrong to this, it just gives you the option to share what you want.

Both clients and contractors can choose to allow their profiles to be searchable on public search engines. This can be a great way to get added exposure, but it all boils down to what you're comfortable with.

The Least You Need to Know

- The quantity of business passing through Elance demands a high standard of protection for both sides of any transaction.
- Use the project agreement templates for added legal protection.
- Check with your CPA and/or lawyer if you have any tax or legal concerns.
- Elance policies are straightforward and designed to protect both sides.
- Use the Privacy Settings page if you want to keep private the amount you've earned or spent.

Managing Your Account—and Your Money

In This Chapter

- Your account setting options
- Making yourself available for job invitations
- Understanding the escrow system
- Elance's Hourly Work Guarantee
- Managing your financial accounts

As your business grows on Elance, you'll be spending a lot of time on the website. Whether as a contractor or client, you'll be opening and closing projects, transferring money, and dealing with the quirks and nuances of any business system or platform. It's best to understand how it works and what your options are for changes.

Just as with your own home or office, take some time to make yourself comfortable in this virtual work world. The escrow system and payment options are designed to create and maintain a stable and secure work environment, as is your ability to easily access your money.

To a certain degree, you can also tailor communication options and make sure you're available for job invitations by the type of clients of your choosing. If you dig, the opportunities expand. I'll show you how.

Really Important Settings to Know

No, this section won't bore you to tears or throw you into a hair-ripping fit of frustration. You actually have a lot of very cool options available to tailor your account so it's as easy to use as possible. Like any traditional office, you can manage and decorate your virtual workspace to your taste.

To access the Settings area, click on your user name in the top-right corner of any Elance page. From the drop-down menu, click on **Settings**. The page that comes up will be full of options, as shown in Figure 15.1.

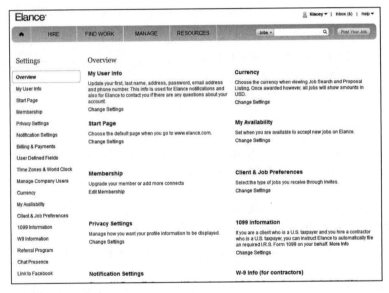

Figure 15.1: *The Settings page gives you myriad options for tailoring your account.*

My User Info

If you haven't figured out where the heck to change your email or how to put in your new address, this is the spot. Click on **My User Info** and—voilà!—the mystery is solved. You can also change your password from here.

Notification Settings

This is an interesting area and will help you organize the communications you receive.

Settings	Notification Settings
Overview	Email the below notifications to the account address: ▓▓▓▓▓ **@gmail.com** [Change Email]
My User Info	**Workroom Messages**
Start Page	
Membership	☑ Immediate email copy of all workroom messages (does not include meeting transcripts).
Privacy Settings	
Notification Settings	☐ Daily email digest of all messages and meeting transcripts (every 24 hours).
Billing & Payments	☐ Send me a confirmation email every time I send an email to a workroom.
User Defined Fields	Optionally send daily email digests and workroom messages selected above to the additional email addresses below (for contractors
Time Zones & World Clock	only, support for clients coming soon):
Manage Company Users	
Currency	
My Availability	Separate email addresses with a comma (maximum 3 email addresses). For example, abc@gmail.com,
Client & Job Preferences	abcW@hotmail.com
1099 Information	**Job Proposal Activity**
W9 Information	
Referral Program	☑ Alert me when there is activity concerning my job proposal (e.g., proposal is declined, hiring period is extended, etc.).
Chat Presence	**Other**
Link to Facebook	
	☑ Elance Newsletter Bi-monthly email containing relevant stories about the Elance community.
	☑ Special Promotions and Offers Notices about special offers for Elance users.

Figure 15.2: *Change how you want to be communicated by Elance from here.*

If you have several projects going on at once, you might want to receive one email per day with all your communication included. This can help manage not only your emails, but also your time. Depending on your individual circumstances, if you reply to emails once per day, this can be a more efficient use of your time rather than being interrupted throughout the day.

TOP TIPS

For contractors and clients alike, the Elance newsletter is a good way to stay abreast of new features and tools Elance has to offer. It also has articles written by Elance members offering tips, stories, and advice.

You can also elect to have your emails sent to more than one person. This can help if you're part of a team and need to make sure all relevant parties are included in the information loop.

You can opt in or out of surveys, special promotions, the Elance newsletter, and even weekly status reports (although I certainly don't recommend opting out of the latter).

My Availability

The My Availability setting (see Figure 15.3) is actually quite important for contractors. When a client posts a job, Elance will suggest potential contractors to be invited based on the job criteria and that client's previous hiring habits. This is great news for contractors as they're now getting invited to more and more jobs.

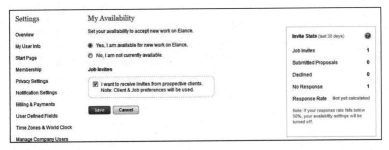

Figure 15.3: *The My Availability setting determines whether or not you'll be sent job invitations by clients.*

However, a few rules exist that you should be well aware of. (Aspects of the Elance search suggestions features are also discussed in Chapters 5 and 10.)

TOP TIPS

Especially for new contractors, it's a good idea to periodically check your My Availability status to make sure you're open for job invitations. You never know where the next job will come from, and it would be a shame to miss out just because one button wasn't clicked.

As a contractor, if you don't respond to a job invitation, it impacts both your Elance level (explained in Chapter 4) and your future chances of more invitations. Within each 30-day period, you must respond to at least 50 percent of your job invitations. If you don't, the formula used to determine your level will be adversely impacted, and you will be automatically established as "Not currently available" for new jobs.

The purpose of this is to keep the invitation process active, and to not pester busy contractors and clients with invitations that aren't going to be responded to. The good news is, even if you decline the invitation, you have responded to it and you won't be negatively judged by the system.

Client & Job Preferences

This is a great little feature. In line with the My Availability option, this setting gives you a choice as to what type of client and job you'd like to receive invitations from. This setting will apply to those invitations based on the results of Elance's own recommendations to clients posting jobs. If a client searches through contractors and decides to invite you, this setting will not restrict them. (That's a good thing.)

You can choose the budget range and whether it's an hourly or a fixed-fee project. And you can sort for a high project award ratio, and the amount of total business the client has done on Elance. Remember, if you sort for high dollar amounts and high award ratios, you will be eliminating invitations from new clients. Think about it, but you have the choice here.

All That Other Stuff

Scroll through the Settings page and see what else might be of value to you. Each person and situation is different, but chances are you'll be able to tailor aspects of your account. Even if not now, you'll know it's here if your situation changes down the road.

Put It in Escrow

For both clients and contractors, Elance's escrow system is one of the favorite features (see Figure 15.4). Just as in buying a home, both sides are protected monetarily until the end result is reached and signed off on by both parties. As the escrow system smoothes the home purchase process, it also smoothes the Elance work environment.

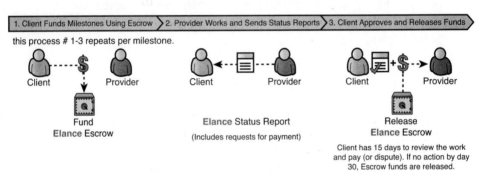

Figure 15.4: *The Elance escrow process.*

The Escrow system is available for fixed fee projects only. (Hourly projects can qualify for the Hourly Work Guarantee.) After the project terms and milestones have been agreed upon, the client can fund the escrow account. She can fund one milestone at a time, or fill them all up right at the outset.

The contractor loves this because he can get to work knowing the client has made the payment(s) and once the work is done the money will be released. The client is satisfied because although she's paid out her funds, they won't actually be released until she's approved the work. Dispute assistance is available if a disagreement arises.

BEST PRACTICES

It's excellent relationship management for clients to proactively fund and release milestone payments. If a contractor has to constantly remind and ask for payments, it leaves a bad taste. Contrarily, if the client proceeds without being asked, the contractor feels valued. This is fertile ground for long-term, mutually beneficial relationships.

When the project terms and milestones are agreed upon by both parties, they will be notified and Elance will send out a request to the client to fund the first milestone. The contractor is not required to begin work without at least one milestone funded, although many times they do so anyway.

Escrow Management for Contractors

To request funding of a milestone by a client, go to your project workroom. Click on **Billing & Invoices** in the left-side menu. Here you are shown each milestone and delivery date, and what has been funded and released from escrow, as shown in Figure 15.5.

Figure 15.5: *The Escrow Funding and Release Status page for contractors.*

To request funding of a milestone, click on the relevant milestone within the Fund Escrow column. To request the release of funds, click on that column.

As well, when you complete a milestone and mark it as complete in your weekly status report, an invoice requesting funding of the next milestone will automatically be generated and sent to the client by Elance.

Escrow Management for Clients

For a client, the management of the escrow system isn't much different than that for a contractor. From the project workroom, click on **Payments** from the left-side menu. This will bring up each milestone agreed upon and the status of the funding and release of escrow funds as in Figure 15.6. Simply click on whichever chunk needs to be taken care of next, and you will be directed through the process by Elance.

PO Number: MA-6710 [edit]				Enter TAX or VAT ID Information
Fund and Release Documents				Pay Bonus/Expense
Milestone | Delivery Date	**Contract Amount**	**Fund Escrow**	**Release Escrow**	
1. November 2011 monthly payment Nov 01, 2011	$2,283.10	✓	✓	
2. Final Deliverable Nov 04, 2011	$2,283.10	✓	✓	
3. December 2011 monthly payment Dec 01, 2011	$2,283.10	✓	✓	
4. January 2012 monthly payment Jan 01, 2012	$2,283.10	Fund	Release	
5. February 2012 monthly payment Feb 01, 2012	$2,283.10	Fund	Release	
6. March 2012 monthly payment Mar 01, 2012	$2,283.10	Fund	Release	

Need to change or add more milestones? Click here.

Figure 15.6: *From the project workroom you can access the escrow Fund and Release section.*

Stopping Payment

Two ways exist to stop the release of escrow funds depending on the nature of the situation. If the contractor and client agree to stop the payment, for whatever reason, the contractor simply clicks on **Void** in the Billing & Invoices page. Only the contractor can do this.

CYBER SNAGS

It's important to pay promptly and fund the next milestone. However, equally, don't pay before the milestone or project has been completed to your satisfaction. Check the work in a timely fashion, then pay.

If there's a dispute over payment, from the project workroom click on **Refund, Cancel or Dispute Job** from the left-side menu. I'll cover handling disputes in detail in Chapter 17.

The client has a 30-day window to release the escrow funds or to dispute them. If she does neither, the funds will be released automatically.

Project Payment Options

Elance provides different payment options for your projects and each comes with its own set of bells and whistles. Like most things, it's best to understand your choices so you can make an educated decision as to what will work best for your unique situation.

Some contractors and clients swear by one payment option, while others are equally adamant about the alternative. The fact is, it all works, it's just a matter of what suits you and the job at hand.

Fixed Fee vs. Hourly Pay

You can work and hire either on a fixed-fee or hourly pay basis within Elance. Fixed fee is where the entire project costs the client a set amount paid to the contractor. With fixed-fee projects, the escrow system, status reports, and milestones are used.

Some clients and contractors prefer this option. They like the fact that the parameters are set and everyone knows what is due by when. When and how often the contractor works is irrelevant as long as the job is done properly.

Continuing work can be done project by project, each with its milestones and end deadline. The parameters are clear with few variables.

However, an equal number of clients and contractors prefer the hourly pay option. Not all jobs lend themselves to a fixed-fee structure. Virtual assistants, marketing positions, and certain design work are some of the possibilities for hourly jobs. Also, sometimes it's just too much of a hassle to keep posting new projects and closing them. It's easier for the same client and contractor to work together on an hourly pay basis.

Milestones are also used for hourly jobs, as is the ability to set a fixed number of authorized hours to work each week. Tracker and Work View can be used for hourly jobs as well as the Guaranteed Payment system, which I'll discuss next. (Tracker and Work View I discuss in detail in Chapter 13.)

Switching a job from fixed fee to hourly or the other way around is simple. Simply click on **Terms & Milestones** in the workroom. Then click on **Change to Hourly Job**, as in Figure 15.7, or **Change to Fixed Fee**, whichever is appropriate.

Figure 15.7: *You can easily switch a job from fixed fee to hourly and vice versa.*

In other words, each avenue for payment has its set of features to ensure the smooth conduct of business. It's a matter of choosing what best suits your personality, business model, and project.

Hourly Work Guarantee

The Hourly Work Guarantee goes hand in hand with Work View and Tracker. Both parties must agree to use Work View and Tracker while working on the specified project. It is only while utilizing these features that the Hourly Work Guarantee comes into play.

Hours billed by the contractor are guaranteed payment as long as they have the proper documentation via the Work View screenshots. If the client disputes the screenshots and the screenshots back him up, the contractor will not be paid for that time. However, if the client disputes the screenshots and yet Elance deems them proper during the dispute process, Elance will guarantee the payment to the contractor.

For many hourly jobs, this is a must. Without Work View and Tracker the contractor isn't assured of payment through Elance, and the client doesn't really know what the contractor has done. If trust has already been established, the two parties can carry on without any of these features. But in the process of establishing a relationship, it really helps to have everything out in the open.

Following the Money

Elance makes it easy and safe to keep track of money spent and earned. After all, in the end the bottom line is the dollar. We're here to live richer and more enlightened lives, but also to make a living, or at least to supplement the one we have.

You can leave money in your Elance account (with no interest added) or transfer it out. All transactions are recorded and you must use your user name and password each time you access your financial data.

Your Financial Accounts

To access your financial accounts, click on **Manage** in the top main toolbar and then on **Financial Accounts** from the drop-down menu. From here you can add or delete a bank account, credit card, or PayPal account.

For non-U.S. residents, you also have the choice of getting a Payoneer Prepaid MasterCard, which works like a debit card on your Elance account. Or you can open a Skrill account for overseas transfers.

Financial Transactions

Each financial transaction you conduct within the Elance system is recorded. This is one of the advantages of always working within the Elance system. Not only is your money safe, but records are kept that you can easily access and download.

TOP TIPS

As your freelancing business grows, be sure to consult with your accountant, CPA, or tax software to determine if you should be paying quarterly estimated taxes. More than one top freelancer has groaned as they realized what they owed and should have been paying already after a successful year.

As your business grows with Elance, these types of details can get lost in the shuffle of paper and life as you get busier and more successful. But everything's here, ready for your perusal. As well, items within your financial history are linked to the project and the invoice details.

Bringing Home the Bacon

Withdrawing funds from Elance is easy and safe. Simply go to **Manage** in the top main toolbar. Next, click on **Withdraw**. Your balance will be clearly displayed as well as your withdrawal options.

You can set up your account to enable transfers directly into your bank or PayPal accounts, or have physical checks sent to you. Expect some delays as funds are cleared, but for the most part withdrawals are handled lickety-split.

Global Payments

All Elance transactions are done in U.S. dollars. However, clients and contractors live and work across the globe. Having a single currency, like using one language, English, as the default, simplifies conducting business enormously.

The Elance platform also supports international transfers. You can conduct bank transfers in U.S. dollars or in your local currency, and you can also use PayPal.

CYBER SNAGS

All transactions done through Elance are in U.S. dollars. If this isn't your home currency, you will be subject to the rise and fall of currency exchange rates. Remember to add this variable to your overall business plan.

To access information on the global payment features, you need to do a bit of monkey work. Scroll down to the bottom of most any page you're working from, and just above the Elance logo click on **Global Payments**. This brings up a plethora of information on accessing your money and transferring it to most anywhere it needs to go.

The Least You Need to Know

- Use the account settings options to tailor your account and make sure you don't get left out of project invitations.
- The escrow feature is easy, safe, and good business practice for both clients and contractors.
- Fixed-fee projects use the escrow, milestones, and status reports.
- Hourly pay projects use milestones, timesheets, allocated weekly hours, and the Tracker and Work View systems.
- The Hourly Work Guarantee can be applied when Work View is also used.
- You can transfer funds out directly to your bank or PayPal account, or have a physical check cut.

Leveraging Your Elance Experience

Chapter 16

In This Chapter

- Learning tips from top Elance contractors and clients
- Ways to get great feedback and ratings
- Marketing yourself through social media and your website

Getting up and running on Elance is just the beginning of your overall journey. You can dabble in the online work world for as long as you like, or you can focus your intent, work smart and hard, and excel within this strange thing called the cloud.

Learning the tips and techniques from successful clients and contractors is a great way to speed up the process. You'll hear conflicting points of view, and you'll land upon ideas you never thought of. The key is to learn from the best, and then apply what works for your personality and situation.

Marketing yourself through feedback, social media, and your business website are also key ingredients to your success. Take it one step at a time if you like, but try to incorporate as many of these tools as you can. The result may just surprise you!

Don't Miss Out

As you learn more about Elance and the contractors and clients involved, you'll begin to notice that some really stand apart from the pack. Certain individuals and businesses take off like rockets as the Elance experience transforms their lives.

The fact is, you can leverage your Elance experience. You can take certain actions to put your online presence in front of more people, whether talented freelancers or clients. The opportunity is immense, but you must position yourself to take advantage. By proactively working toward higher goals, it's these very same lofty levels that you can reach.

The key is to work smart and to assess what you've done already. Rather than using a shotgun approach and scattering tiny hits everywhere, it's better to focus on what's working and how you can improve what's not. If you take the time to study your online business, you'll see avenues where you can make a difference. It's refining these that will help you excel.

Remember, success isn't achieved by analyzing your business once in the beginning and then sticking it on autopilot. It's a matter of continually figuring out the good and not-so-good areas, and honing the formula. Big and little changes will occur, and more than once. Let's look at how you can rev up your business.

Following the Footsteps

One of the best ways of all to leverage your Elance experience is to learn from those who have already succeeded. You don't have to reinvent the wheel. If you pay attention to those before you who've made it work, you can shortcut your own learning curve. While everyone's situation is different, many tools, techniques, and mindsets will be transferable to your own situation.

BEST PRACTICES

As you grow your business on Elance, you will develop your own network of Elancers that you can exchange ideas and best practices with. Nurture these relationships for both what you can teach and what you can learn.

Following are the stories and circumstances of several clients and contractors who've found extraordinary success with Elance. Many more stories exist, but each of these carries something that I hope you can learn from and apply to your own virtual work world.

Top Clients

I'll begin with the real stories of three clients. Each explains where they were before hiring online became a factor, and where they ended up afterward.

Try to see how their circumstances might mirror yours and what you can take away. Contractors should read these stories as well. It's always important to see things from the other person's side. This increases the level of understanding and therefore communication. When communication is increased, so is the personal connection. And connection, dear reader, is what it's all about.

Ken Lancaster

Ken is the owner of Lancaster Advertising based in Lewisville, Texas (www.lancasteradvertising.com). Before he tapped into the virtual work world, he had a traditional company with full-time staff, two office buildings, and a steady flow of red ink from his balance sheet.

He discovered Elance through a single catalog project that had gone awry. The client had changed his mind about the background for the photography in the catalog just before it was due to go to press. Someone was going to have to quickly go in and make adjustments on thousands of parts.

BEST PRACTICES

Ken Lancaster emphasizes that as a client, you are competing for the best contractors. English may not be their first language, so make your project easy to understand, and remain friendly and professional at all times.

In Ken's words, "I knew that any designer on my staff I assigned the project to would simply quit. And the project was already too far behind to afford the $8,000 to $10,000 of local freelance help it would take to get someone to do the work. Elance to the rescue. I hired a Photoshop-certified service provider in Romania. He was better at Photoshop than anyone on my staff. He did the work in two weeks and charged me $600. Needless to say, I was impressed."

Ken gradually changed his business model to include more freelancers from Elance and fewer local hires. He found he had more talent to choose from, and was able to get his projects done quickly at a lower cost.

Ken has done over 400 projects with Elance, has spent about $170,000 on freelancers, and can work from home, his office, or the local coffee shop.

His best advice to a new Elance client is the following:

- Write concise and complete project descriptions. Detail here saves you time, money, and hassle down the road.

- Hire full-time freelancers who have an average feedback rating of 4.9 or 5.0.

- Hire freelancers who commonly do the type of work you need.

- Make sure you've discussed the project's details and everything you need done and by when, *before* you click the **Award** button and hire your freelancer.

- Be nice. It goes a long way.

Ken has had several freelancers thank him for the difference he's made in their lives. One even sent him a picture of the house he was able to buy because of the business he'd done with Ken. That's win-win.

BEST PRACTICES

Many clients use outside software, such as Microsoft Excel, to help manage their Elance projects. This keeps the current projects separate yet within set parameters, but also provides a history of each project. You can use this to refine future jobs and to list the contractors that stood out.

Steffen Hedebrandt

Steffen lives in Denmark where the food and culture are wondrous, but the cost of labor will put a kink in the best of business plans. According to Steffen, he simply could not have grown his dream business of selling vintage, rare, and antique musical instruments without the help of hiring online through Elance. (Visit his website at www.vintageandrare.com.)

As COO of Vintage and Rare, when Steffen steps into his virtual office every morning (i.e., his Elance workrooms), he visits with his graphic designer and market researcher, both in India; his social media expert in Pakistan; an SEO specialist in Bulgaria; and a sales and marketing team from Florida. This is leveraging the Elance experience.

Steffen began with a disadvantage—the high cost of labor in his home country—but because of the global talent he discovered on Elance, he overcame this disadvantage and his business is thriving.

Steffen's best practices for new clients are:

- Create quality, clear descriptions of your jobs. (Have you noticed how many clients refer to this?)

- Trust the person you hire and know they are an expert in their field.

- Start with small and simple projects until you get used to working with Elance.

- If you're not an expert in what you're looking to hire for, go into your own community to find someone who is. Maybe a friend or family member or someone referred by them will agree to advise you. Get them to check your job description to make sure it's spot on, and even ask them to help you assess your short list of contractors for the final hiring decision.

Steffen found that hiring in the virtual work world helped him realize his dream and passion. He's tapped into a wealth of talent and a new community of like-minded entrepreneurs. He did this by tearing down the mental boundaries of where he lived, and instead reaching out across the entire world for those who could help.

Ramon Ray

Ramon provides a classic example of leveraging with Elance. He's the owner of a media company called SmallBizTechnology. Ramon's company produces events, provides content, and Ramon speaks at events across the United States. Very simply, Ramon says, "Elance is my talent agency."

> **BEST PRACTICES**
>
> If you don't get a good vibe from a contractor when you begin working with them, you are not stuck but can cancel the project. Sometimes this is a better option than continuing down a path that your intuition is screaming for you not to follow.

Because of the nature of his business, Ramon found that he needed to be in more than one place at once. He just couldn't run his business and be everywhere he needed to be to get the growth he was looking for. But after he dove into the pool of online talent, this all began to change.

Ramon began by hiring a team of writers and then a managing writer to handle the team. His team of Elancers allowed him to significantly raise his content volume, and therefore he's effectively leveraged his output.

When he puts on an event, he hires Elancers from that geographic region. This way he can have a PR person and an event manager in San Francisco, while he's working a different event in Chicago. He can use Elance to leverage himself geographically.

He says that he likes Elance because he can hire people who are smart. In his words, "I can't be there and I need to be able to trust who I hire. I want the hire to be more expensive because I need the quality. I need to be able to trust them."

Ramon also says, "You never know what else you can do. I can now do an infographic just like the big boys if I want. Small movie? Why not? I can compete now that I know where to find the people to hire."

His best practices for new clients are:

- Test freelancers with small projects first. If you get along, you can hire them again.

- Be clear in the terms you use; a blogger is not necessarily the same as a freelance writer, for example.

- For larger groups of freelancers, use one as the overall manager.

- Don't play around; the contractors are people, too.

- Establishing trust is crucial.

By leveraging his company through Elance, Ramon has been able to build his business while working from home. He's achieved a lifestyle he never could have achieved with the traditional brick-and-mortar business model. (Visit Ramon's website at www.smallbiztechnology. com.)

Top Contractors

The life of the freelancer isn't for everyone. It takes a special personality to give up the security of a steady paycheck for the luxury of being your own boss. Sometimes the process isn't voluntary. With the amount of corporate layoffs and downsizings over the past years, more and more people have found themselves needing to bring in that extra income.

What often happens is that people give freelancing a try first. They take on a few jobs, get the feel for it, and then decide if it's a fit. The thing is, many blossom in this environment. The following three stories illustrate such success.

Julie Babikin

Julie was laid off from her job with a financial services company and left with no way to pay her mortgage. She lived 45 minutes from the city, was exhausted from commuting, and no one in her local area was hiring graphic designers of her level. "You're overqualified," they kept telling her.

Julie began investigating where other designers who'd been laid off were working and discovered the cloud. Elance looked like the most reputable of the sites, and she dug in. Within a year she was not only making more money than when she worked for a traditional company, but she worked from home and had the luxury of setting her own schedule and only choosing projects that she wanted.

Julie's best advice for budding freelancers is:

- The best clients clearly spell out their project needs.

- Don't bid on just any job; pick those you really want to do. Your passion will come out this way.

- Don't underbid, or clients (good ones) will wonder why you don't value yourself.

- The best clients to work for are those that pick you for your portfolio or proposal, not your price.

- A great proposal involves a plan of action.

- After you've placed your bid but before the prospective client has awarded the job, ask them a question by resubmitting your proposal.

- Play on their style. If they're edgier, you can be bolder in your bid or use humor.

Julie turned her unexpected and negative experience—being laid off—into a positive outcome by tapping into the virtual work world. It didn't happen overnight, but by working smart and hard, she turned her world around for the better. You can find Julie on Elance as animatorjb or Julie B.

Khrystyne Robillard-Smith

Khrystyne was laid off from her job while seven months pregnant. Her husband suggested she try Elance as a way to supplement their income until she was able to look for full-time work again. However, once Khrystyne discovered the online work world it didn't take her long to realize the potential here was far greater than she'd ever find in the brick-and-mortar world.

On Elance, Khrystyne is the number one individual designer out of more than 100,000. How on earth did she achieve this staggering success? In her own words:

> "In the beginning my selection process was to bid on anything I thought I could do for a price I could live with. At one point I tried bidding on all jobs that ended soonest, most of which turned out to be stale and never got awarded. So I learned you gotta get 'em when they're fresh.
>
> I bought additional Connects so that I could bid more volume as well. The result was that I would sometimes end up doing work I wasn't crazy about for what ended up being way too low a price.
>
> It took me about a year and a half to really look at the site and analyze it to improve this scenario. I spent time looking into the clients' profiles and feedback, as well as my competition—especially those I continually lost projects to. Were they beating me on price? On experience? Whose portfolios seemed as qualified as mine? What made others better?
>
> I also started researching standard projects like logos. How much were they selling for on the site? And what types of things was the client looking for at those price points? It was a lot of tedious, hard work, but patterns started to emerge, and that information led me to make more informed decisions on what projects I'd bid on in the future.
>
> Once I unlocked those key points and how they applied to me, doors started opening. There's a lot of room working in the cloud, I just needed to find the right spot for me."

Khrystyne's advice for newcomers is:

- Have passion for what you do. Clients can tell when you're genuine.

- Don't undersell yourself.

- Take the time to thoughtfully fill out your profile and portfolio.

- Be tenacious. It takes time and effort to build your brand.

- Don't do any spec work or contests. Working for free devalues the site and the industry as a whole.

TOP TIPS

If a client asks you to lower your price, tell them no, politely. You are lowering your value and that of the services you provide. An alternative is to agree to the lower price, but to have them take something away from the project requirements, too.

Khrystyne didn't sit idly by and hope for good luck. She proactively studied the site and learned how she could best fit in with the services she wanted to provide. In the end, it worked out better than even she expected. You can find Khrystyne on Elance as Khrystyne R, and at her website, www.713creative.com.

TOP TIPS

Don't be scared or intimidated to submit your first proposal. Every contractor has done it. It's like jumping into a cool lake, after the initial plunge you warm up and swim like you've been there your entire life.

Ron Zvagelsky

Ron began his freelancing career as a Wordpress expert just after graduating from college. Broke and still living at home, Ron knew he needed to make a change, but finding a job proved difficult in these hard economic times.

He discovered Elance and within a year became successful enough to get his own place and fully support himself. He has now done more than 400 jobs on Elance over the course of four years and has more work than he can handle.

Ron's best practices include:

- When you bid on a project and don't win it, check in to see who did win and how they differed from you.

- The best clients know what they want and communicate their needs clearly.

- If the project's price range is under your budget, throw out a feeler question to see if they'll go up in price.

- As you get more work and establish yourself, assess each project as to whether it was worth your time or not. This will help you set your prices.

- Ask questions in the bidding process to get the communication going—even if you know the answers.

- Follow up with your client after the work is done to make sure they're happy. You never know where the next referral will come from.

- The most important thing you need to do is create the relationship with the client.

- Keep going; keep putting out proposals. Don't take rejection personally.

Ron's persistence and focus on connecting with the client have led him to receive astounding referrals. It's all about the relationship, which includes delivering on the goods until the client is happy. You can find Ron on Elance as rzvagelsky, and on his website at www. presshive.com.

CYBER SNAGS

Remember, clients are busy, too. "I'll give you more work just as soon as I get it" should be taken as polite, but not as a guarantee. Keep moving. Keep bidding.

Crucial Feedback and Ratings

Let's zero in on some of the more specific areas that will help leverage your experience. Feedback and ratings is the area most commonly referenced by contractors and clients when assessing working together. Think about it, if someone tells you they had a great business experience with someone—be it a dentist, mechanic, architect, hair stylist, whomever—you're much more likely to use their services yourself.

> **TOP TIPS**
>
> Being *recommended* by a client is different from getting a five-star rating. Both are good, but clients state whether or not they would recommend a contractor in a separate area in the feedback process.

Many people won't work with an unknown, they'll simply wait until they find someone recommended. It's human nature. In these situations, we trust what people tell us and it affects our decision making.

As a client or contractor on Elance, you get to turn this fact into an advantage. By concentrating on and working on improving your personal feedback and ratings, you can build up this crucial self-advertising tool.

Ask for It

Plain and simple, if you ask for it you get it, most of the time. Contractors need to step up and ask for feedback, as do clients. It works both ways. The logic on both sides is the same, positive feedback as a contractor/client helps you get more work or more top talent.

Asking for feedback doesn't mean to manipulate anyone or to make some kind of deal on the side. It's the natural progression from a job well done, and it's part of the Elance process. If you have to finagle to get good feedback, you're not going to last long anyway. Half-hearted or downright dishonest members will eventually be outed by other members in the form of negative feedback and ratings.

Set the Example

Whether contractor or client, you can be the first one to submit feedback and set the example for the other party. As a contractor, you take on a slight risk if the client wasn't completely happy and you've already said how wonderful they were. But for the most part, this is a great way to lead.

After the job is completed, the Elance system will send a reminder to both the client and contractor to submit feedback within 60 days. Consider getting a head start and being the first to type in positive remarks. Then let your client/contractor know and ask them to give you feedback, too.

What to Do with Bad Feedback

Inevitably, you will receive less than stellar feedback from someone. Personalities clashed, the job parameters needed to change, or it just didn't flow as smoothly as everyone would have liked. It happens.

BEST PRACTICES

Don't ever mislead with feedback. If the contractor didn't do a great job, say so. It's the best way to keep the Elance environment clean and of high quality. But also don't be a nitpicker. No project goes perfectly and you shouldn't penalize your contractor for that. Overall, did they do what they claimed they were going to do in a timely fashion? Did they stay within budget? Was the end result what you wanted? If so, give 'em the good stuff.

As a contractor, when you get negative feedback, or even if it's less positive than you expected, you have a chance to reply and voice your side of the story. As you peruse feedback left for contractors and clients, you will periodically run across these exchanges.

One-offs are not that big a deal. Yes, they're aggravating, especially if you feel slighted and that the feedback was unjust. After all, it does lower your overall averages. But it's also life.

Submit your response to what the client wrote remembering to always be clear, professional, and polite. Save what you really want to say for family and friends. Online you are representing your professionalism. Yes, defend yourself, but no, don't lower into a tit for tat.

Prospective clients will understand that issues happen and if they're not a regular occurrence, they're not a problem. If you're consistently getting negative feedback, you most definitely need to look at yourself and the services you're providing.

For clients, contractors rarely leave negative feedback unless defending themselves. Contractors are more at the mercy of feedback than clients are.

Marketing Yourself

Some of you are natural marketers. You instinctively understand how to put yourself in front of people who can help you and don't hesitate to do it. You're up-to-date on all the latest gadgets and thingamajigs that can help you get your name out.

CYBER SNAGS

If you're not a marketing and social media natural, don't go throwing yourself into these endeavors all at once. You may get frustrated and burnt out wondering how you actually veered away from your dream life rather than getting closer to it. Rather, take it one chunk at a time. Start with building a professional website or signing up on Twitter and let that sink in before you take on the next marketing angle.

Others would rather crawl in a hole and hang out with the shrews than promote themselves. Talking to strangers about yourself and your services is awkward and something you only do at virtual gunpoint.

Fortunately for both types of people, vehicles exist to make marketing yourself easier. It's a fact that if you want your business to grow, more and more people need to know about it. You can rely solely on feedback and proposals, but you can also kick the process in the behind and get quicker results.

Social Media and Elance

Facebook, Twitter, Linked In, YouTube, and other social media venues are a great way to spread the word about what you do. Due to the "social" nature of many of these, you can also spread the news in a friendly and casual way. This helps alleviate the stress associated with promoting yourself that many people experience.

It's pretty easy to link your Elance presence with social media outlets. You can post your profile on your Facebook page as well as let folks know of any new jobs you've taken on. This is a way to celebrate the new work, as well as to spread the word about what you do. You just never know where the next referral will come from.

When you post a project, you are automatically asked if you would like to post it on your Facebook page. You can also Tweet about it or upload it to Linked In.

If you're new to the world of social media, get involved step by step. If you're an old hand, then proactively use these tools to get the word out about what you do. Don't pummel people with it, but instead regularly update them on what you're doing. Most of the time people are fascinated with this online work thing and want to know more.

You Don't Have a Website?

Really? Okay, I have to lay down the law here. You must get a website. Now.

Whether a contractor or client, if you intend on growing your business you need to have a website. This is where you continue to promote your services, let people know who you are and what you're up to, and nurture that precious human connection.

It doesn't need to be fancy. You can have a streamlined and simple site, or one with as many bells and whistles as you can stand. The fact is your website is a crucial link in your marketing process.

BEST PRACTICES

Many top clients say they always check out a potential contractor's website as yet another gauge as to how professional the freelancer is. If they don't have a site, or it's shoddy and out-of-date, that's a red flag when the client is building his short list.

You can easily embed your Elance profile right on your website. To do this, go to **Resources** on the main top toolbar and click on **Widgets & Tools**. From here you can download the Elance Profile Widget (Figure 16.1), which will place your profile in your website.

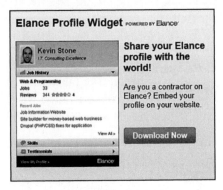

Figure 16.1: *The Elance Profile Widget embeds your Elance profile within your website.*

If you're a do-it-yourselfer, you can build your own website without too much turmoil. Or you can always hire an Elance contractor to do the job for you. This is a great alternative as you get quality talent working on your behalf, but you also get a close look at what it's like to hire and work with someone within the Elance system. This alone is worth the price of building a website.

The Least You Need to Know

- Top clients consistently say to write clear project descriptions, start with small jobs first, and always be fair and professional.
- Consistent advice from top contractors is to write targeted, clear proposals; never underbid and lower your value; and choose those jobs you're passionate about.
- Work toward getting positive feedback and ratings.
- Create a professional website and use social media, such as Facebook and Twitter, to leverage your marketing potential.

Troubleshooting Guide

In This Chapter

- Rules to avoid breaking
- What to do if you really mess up
- How to get your money back
- Canceling or disputing a project
- Steps to work together to resolve misunderstandings

For the most part, the Elance work environment runs smoothly. Fewer than 1 percent of all projects require dispute assistance. Communicating is easy through workroom messaging, the money is safe in escrow, and barring the normal quirks and foibles of any work experience, business is conducted with few if any hitches.

However, sometimes stuff happens. In these cases, it's important for you to understand what resources and recourses you have to rectify the issue. Some, you will need to drum up within your own personality and conflict-resolving tools. Others, Elance provides. Both should suffice to make sure that your journey through Elance-land is as trouble free as possible.

Remember that the best way to solve problems is to avoid them in the first place. Learn how to manage the technical aspects of the system—and for the most part Elance walks you through this—and always communicate clearly. Repeat yourself if necessary, and do so politely. Most issues can be avoided this way.

Breaking the Rules

Elance has certain rules, and if you break them Elance can come in and close your account. The idea isn't that they're Big Brother and will come swooping down when you don't sing the Party song. It's that the goal is to have a safe and professional environment within which to conduct business.

Creating this environment means having and enforcing certain rules. Chief among these is to not accept payment outside of the Elance system. The entire structure breaks down if you do this, and Elance will close you down fast. To get reinstated, if possible, you will have to jump through hoops.

The interesting part about this is, you're actually safer using the Elance payment system even though it costs contractors up to 8.75 percent per transaction. Nothing can tear up a relationship like money can—ask any family dividing up an estate. In the business environment it's the same.

TOP TIPS

If you are a contractor and not feeling comfortable in the working relationship you have with a client, you can always call the Elance help desk and ask them what you can do. Maybe you've got to stick it out, but maybe not. There's usually a way to work through, or out of, a difficult situation.

I had been living in Buenos Aires, Argentina, for about five months when I got an email from Elance saying that if I didn't prove my residency I would have my account closed. I'd been working on Elance the entire time I was traveling but had no idea what the problem with my account might be.

It turned out Elance had picked up that I wasn't conducting business from the same IP address that I had signed up on. This is one way they make sure that whoever signs up for the account is actually the person doing the work.

Not knowing what was going on, I Skyped Elance, explained my situation, and was told that if I stayed in Buenos Aires I would have to change the home location in my profile. Even when I explained I was flying home soon to live and work, they still required that I send them a photocopy of my driver's license to prove my residence. Elance is watching ….

I have also seen them close projects because the contractors were asked to provide free editing or writing in order to determine who was best for the job. Another big no-no, and rightfully so.

In the future, expect more innovation in ensuring both contractors and clients are who they say they are. This is crucial for maintaining a safe and quality work environment.

Oops, I Did What?

Another category of troubleshooting is required when we actually shoot ourselves in the virtual foot. We might release funds from escrow when we didn't mean to, or forget to turn on Work View when we begin the day's project. I once had someone send me the wrong manuscript to edit and then they disappeared for two months.

In these cases where you or the person you are working with has made a mistake, the best way to solve the problem is to first contact the other party and explain the situation. If this doesn't resolve the issue, take it up a step by contacting Elance.

> **BEST PRACTICES**
>
> As a client, you have more clout because you control the money in the project. Given this and the end goal of long-term mutually beneficial relationships, give the contractor the benefit of the doubt until proven otherwise. Mistakes and misunderstandings happen; stick with innocent-until-proven-guilty unless you have a really strong gut feeling about it.

If you released funds from escrow when you didn't mean to, let the contractor know and either ask them to refund the money or make it clear that this payment is not in acknowledgment of the work being completed. Nine times out of 10 the contractor will understand and the issue will be resolved.

The outcome of these types of mistakes depends on you and the relationship you have with the other party. Again, the better the relationship, the easier these knots work out. In my case with the wrong manuscript, I simply waited the two months until the client returned and then we canceled the project.

If you are a contractor and forget to turn on Work View, you are reliant on the goodwill of the client to believe you and pay for the time. Lesson learned: always turn on Work View. You can dispute the issue with Elance, but you're stuck in a situation where you aren't able to prove you were working.

Refund, Cancel or Dispute

At the bottom of the menu on the left of each project's workroom, you will find the option of Refund, Cancel or Dispute, as shown in Figure 17.1. As the title implies, this is where you will go if talking through an issue with your client or contractor leads to less than satisfactory results.

Figure 17.1: *Elance provides Refund, Cancel or Dispute features from the left-hand menu in each workroom.*

It is from the Refund, Cancel or Dispute page that you can take the problematic issue to the next level (see Figure 17.2). Each party is given the opportunity to agree with the other's request. If they don't do so, one or both parties can elect Elance's arbitration facility.

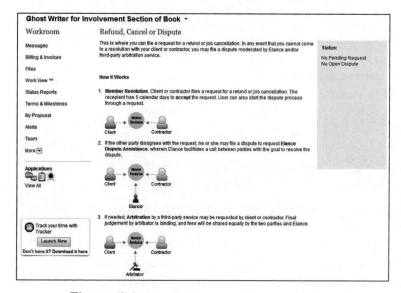

Figure 17.2: *The Refund, Cancel or Dispute process.*

Refunding Payments

For a client to ask the contractor to refund a payment, you have a couple of options. You can go to the Refund, Cancel or Dispute page, scroll to the bottom and click on **File a Request**. This will bring up a page with your three choices as in Figure 17.3. Whichever one you click on will start that process and Elance will guide you through it.

 CYBER SNAGS

Disputes are rare, but if they happen you'll be very glad you kept good records and communicated clearly and often through Elance's work-room message board. Elance's dispute-resolution process only reviews communication from here. You did that, right?

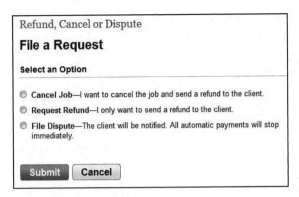

Figure 17.3: *Filing a request.*

For a contractor to refund a payment to the client, click on **Request Refund**. The system will lead you through the process including filling out a form explaining the reason for the refund.

Either party can also request a refund through the Terms & Milestones page. Go to the main workroom and click on **Terms & Milestones**. If the money is still held in escrow, all you have to do is click on **Edit** next to that payment, change the details, and click **Submit**. The funds will automatically be transferred out of escrow and back to the client.

If the client has actually paid you, the contractor, and you need to refund him, then you must do so through the Refund, Cancel or Dispute page. You can also get to this page from Terms & Milestones. You'll find the link at the top right of the page.

Canceling Projects

Either the client or contractor can cancel the job at any point in time. Obviously, the earlier this is done the cleaner the break. To cancel a project, go to the Refund, Cancel or Dispute page and click on **File a Request**. Next, click on **Cancel Job**.

The cancellation request is sent to the other party and asks them for their approval. When this is received, the job will be canceled and any funds in escrow will be returned to the client. If either side disputes the cancellation, the issue can be escalated up to the arbitration service.

Project Disputes

Three levels exist to the project dispute-resolution process. Initially, go to Refund, Cancel or Dispute, click on **File a Request**, and then **File Dispute**. You'll be asked to fill out a form with all the details of the dispute. This will be sent to the other party. The client and contractor can work out their dispute here.

If the dispute isn't resolved here, it then goes to the Elance Dispute Assistance feature. This entails a phone call between all parties and an Elance representative. Elance won't make a judgment on the situation, but simply try to get the two parties to agree on a resolution.

CYBER SNAGS

Disputes are rare with Elance, and those that go all the way to arbitration even rarer. However, it's good to know what your options are. If there is a problem, you do have recourse. Most Elancers will never use this service.

If the Dispute Assistance call doesn't work, the issue can then go to arbitration. Either party can request this and Elance will use a third party to do the arbitrating. It's non-appearance-based, which makes sense, and both sides will be bound by the results.

A cost is associated with the arbitration process, which is split three ways between Elance, the contractor, and the client. Currently, it's $299 for jobs under $1,000, and $599 for jobs over $1,000.

Getting Back on Track

Most of the time, with a bit of effort and common sense, projects that have been derailed can get back on track for at least the duration of the job, if not for future business. It's a better solution to resolve issues amicably.

The vast majority of the time, project dissatisfaction comes as a result of a lack of communication. A lack of communication leads to false expectations, and this can happen on either side or both. The culprit, therefore, is also the solution.

You can get projects back on track, and you can end up with a job where each party is completely satisfied with the results. But when you see it veering to the side, you must communicate to get it back on track. Don't just let it take off on a trajectory of its own.

Project Posting and Proposal

The first step is to alert the other side that there's an issue broiling. Sometimes this alone will be enough. Simply airing it out will get everyone aligned again.

Go to the original project posting by the client and the proposal by the contractor. Both sides need to review these. Sometimes we think we're being deeply wronged when it turns out we are the ones who misunderstood in the first place. Check out the posting and proposal and write out what was agreed upon.

Review all workroom messages and emails sent before the project was awarded. Sometimes conditions and agreements will have changed in this phase of communication and one side or the other forgot or misunderstood. Add these to the overall picture that you're outlining.

It's best to start by going back to what was originally discussed and agreed upon. This is often exactly where the issue is nesting and you need to smoke it out. It's not a big deal and is easy to do. Obviously, some projects are more complicated than others, but they all will have key deliverables and parameters.

If you find the problem here, great. Job well done. Communicate clearly and politely with the other party. If it's their fault, don't grind it in, just clarify what was agreed upon. If it's your fault, apologize, reaffirm what's expected, and move on.

Workroom Messages, Terms and Milestones, and Agreements

If the project is still stuck, review all your workroom messages, the terms and milestones, and legal agreements signed. Projects aren't always static with fixed deliverables. Go over what you discussed in your workroom messages along the way. You'll be amazed at what might pop up here.

Especially over the course of a lengthy project, a lot will be communicated during the process. This underscores the good idea to always use the workroom message board. Scroll through and remind yourself of what was said. Factors can change and they may appear here.

Also review the terms and milestones you both agreed upon. If you're a client and the contractor hasn't reached one yet, but has moved on as if she has, you need to point this out. If you're the contractor and have done everything you were supposed to but the client is balking on paying, point this out. It's hard to argue with something in writing.

Save, Save, Save

If you use email outside of Elance's messaging system, make sure you save everything. Create a file specifically for this purpose. Save any agreements you exchanged outside of the system.

Also, save any discarded versions of design work or rough drafts of writing projects. These can be useful in demonstrating the work you've done but perhaps are not being given credit for, even though it is not allowed in the Elance dispute process.

A good idea is if you are using private email, cut and paste any relevant information into the workroom message board and ask the other party to confirm it. This way it will be allowed as evidence in any dispute. To save all this hassle? Just stick with workroom messaging and file sharing through Elance.

> **TOP TIPS**
>
> As a contractor, consider keeping a file specifically devoted to completed Elance projects. Here, keep everything that was communicated outside of Elance from each project, and copies of each draft or version that might apply. If a misunderstanding should ever arise in the future, your proverbial ducks will be in a row.

In a nutshell, if it has to do with the project, save it. When you're done and everyone's happy, reconsider what to do with the material. Being organized in this way can save you time and hassle down the road.

The Higher Road

Whatever the depth or cause of your dispute, remember to always remain professional and polite. It doesn't help the overall situation and certainly doesn't help your side to lose your temper or be rude. After all, the end goal is to get the job done. If you become a real pain, no one's going to want to help.

You attract more flies with honey than vinegar. You resolve more disputes with professionalism and communication than with irritability and vitriol. Strength is fine, but bad manners or impolite behavior are not.

Contacting Elance

Elance has a support team that is available to answer questions and help troubleshoot any issues for you. You can access Elance Support by clicking on **Help** in the upper-right menu, as shown in Figure 17.4.

This will bring up a page with several different options, many of which will loop you back into the general Help system. This is fine, but will only refer you to articles written to answer questions.

Figure 17.4: *Contacting Elance Support.*

If you're looking for a real person to answer your questions, you have a couple of ways of going about this. You can click on **Submit a Request** at the top of the Elance Support page. You will then be able to type in your questions and wait for a response. They're pretty good about getting back to you quickly.

Or you can click on the **Live Chat** button and get immediate help.

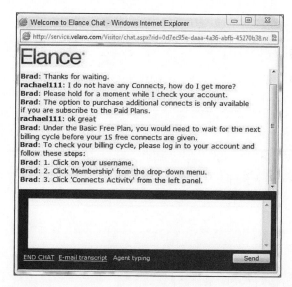

Figure 17.5: *For immediate access to help, you can use the Live Chat facility.*

Most of us would like to get the question answered as quickly as possible and by a real person, and this is a great way to do that.

You can also get Elance by phone. When you post a project, the help number is right there in the upper-right corner of the screen. Otherwise, scroll to the bottom of any page and click on **About** in the footer links. This will take you to all Elance's contact information.

The Least You Need to Know

- Elance can and will close your account if you break certain rules.
- If you just plain mess up, most of the time you can rectify it.
- Be familiar with the process for refunding payments, canceling jobs, or disputing issues.
- Rectify disputes yourself by reviewing and clarifying what you've already agreed upon.
- Use the Live Chat service for immediate help.

The Elance Community

In This Chapter

- The growing Elance community
- Where to interact with other Elance members
- Health insurance options
- Elance's referral programs
- Training videos that cover the basics of Elance

Hundreds of thousands of people have joined the Elance community as clients and/or contractors. Growth on Elance and in this sector is phenomenal and shows no sign of slowing. It makes sense, too. With a stagnant world economy, work still goes on, just in a different way. A more flexible and creative way.

What this means for you is not only are you not alone in this community, but you're part of an exciting new worldwide trend. I've included stories and advice from successful clients and contractors in this book because there's always something you can learn from someone else, especially when they've already figured it out.

The learning doesn't need to stop with this book. You now have the knowledge and tools to achieve your goals with Elance. If you apply what you learned here and mix it with a good dose of elbow grease, nothing will stand in your way. But there's always more to learn, especially when technology is involved. Stay involved, keep up to date, and read on!

You're Not Alone

Not only does Elance support and promote a community of its own, but you will also develop your own network of clients and/or contractors.

Cathy Reed has been a successful writer on Elance for several years. She's worked for clients from 35 countries during this time. Not only does she have an interesting and varied network providing her repeat business and referrals, but she has a window into their own worlds, whether China, Russia, Africa, or the Middle East.

It's these types of hidden benefits that keep you in good company throughout your experience. I have made lifelong business partners and friends through Elance, and these connections have opened up doors I never dreamed of when I began.

The key is you must nurture these relationships and experiences. You may not directly know that Juana from Argentina will end up introducing you to Mark from LA, who offers you a long-term free-lancing job. But if you stick with it, these things can happen.

CYBER SNAGS

As much as you can learn from other Elance members, it's crucial to filter out negativity. Learn, yes; place blame, criticize, and drag other people down, no. Life is hard—for all of us. Surround yourself with positive, creative people and you will reap the mutual benefits.

You can also develop relationships and exchange views, experiences, and opinions with other Elancers through Elance's own set of resources. The virtual work world is just that, a world opened up for you that's full of people and experiences. All you need to do is grasp the opportunity and run with it.

Hot Spots

Hover your mouse over **Resources** in the main top toolbar, and the drop-down menu will provide you with a variety of choices. For this chapter, the ones we're interested in are Special Offers, Blogs, Elance University, Referral Program, and the Water Cooler.

These are places you should return to regularly for new information. Make it a habit once a month to click through these features and see what's new and what you can learn. Over time, this will add to your arsenal of productive ideas and contacts.

The Elance Blog

Locate the Elance blog through the Resources drop-down menu or the footer on each page. Within the blog you will find a plethora of good ideas and advice from Elance members and staff. Articles are regularly posted here, and often they're written by contractors and clients. It's good practice to visit the blog frequently.

You can find great tips and practical advice, and you can comment and receive responses from the author. When new applications or tools are rolled out, you will read about them here.

BEST PRACTICES

Success stories provide glimpses into how other people harnessed the virtual work world. Hunt these down on the blog and study them for what can apply to you. Not everything will, but the ideas that do are priceless.

Also, use the blog search mechanism and blog topics box to locate articles that will help you on whatever questions you want answered. The range of subjects is high and the archive goes back several years. You can also offer to write a blog article yourself, which is a great way to give back to the community.

The Water Cooler

The Water Cooler, shown in Figure 18.1, is a unique and colorful feature mainly used by contractors and some clients. This is where members can actively post comments, opinions, and questions and other Elancers and staff members will respond. It can get lively and sometimes heated, so be prepared.

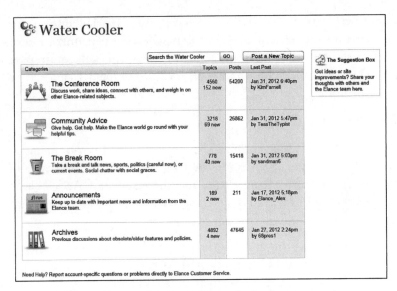

Figure 18.1: *The Water Cooler forum.*

To get here, hover your mouse over **Resources** in the main toolbar and click on **Water Cooler**. Here you will have a menu of choices for places to learn and exchange information.

Check out the areas where Elance members go to discuss the issues of the day. Post your own question or comment, or respond to others. You can get a strong community feeling if you spend much time here. Certain people regularly post and others less frequently, but it's a great place to shake off the cyber-loneliness that can sometimes lurk.

The Water Cooler is also where Elancers vent with few restrictions. You can learn a lot, but you can also get sucked into time-wasting complaining and dead ends. Tread carefully.

Health Insurance

A shared challenge amongst freelancers and small business owners in the United States is the cost of health insurance. If you don't have a large corporation's pool of insurance to join, you can experience a serious dent in your monthly income.

So far, there is no real solution to this conundrum. Maybe you can piggyback on your spouse's insurance, maybe not. You might be the sole or main breadwinner in the family. However, Elance provides a link to eHealth Insurance (see Figure 18.2), a company that offers to help you find the best health insurance options.

Figure 18.2: *Under Special Offers in the Resource section, eHealth Insurance provides quotes for health insurance from different companies.*

TOP TIPS

As you begin your freelancing career, budgets can be tight and income low. Click through the Special Offers section to see if anything here can give you an extra edge as you grow.

Click on **Special Offers** in the Resources drop-down menu and you come up with a series of useful perks.

You may not find the perfect health insurance match, but this is a great place to start looking. You can filter for the specific insurance company, the amount of monthly premium, the deductible, and other features. It's well worth a look.

Professional Perks

Elance knows that word of mouth is one of the best forms of advertising. Because of this, they're willing to reward you for bringing in new business. It makes sense. New clients and contractors make them money, and they pay you for the introduction.

Affiliates Program

Scroll to the bottom of most any page on Elance and you will find links at the footer. Click on **Affiliates Program**. This will take you to the Affiliates Program page where you can view the details and sign up (see Figure 18.3).

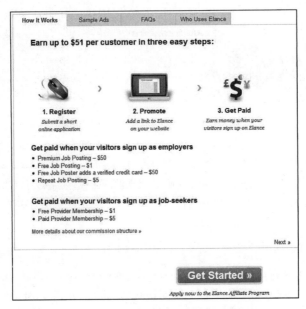

Figure 18.3: *By inserting an Elance ad link in your website, you can earn money when people sign up for Elance through you.*

It's simply a matter of completing a short online application. Once your application is approved, you will have access to text links and banner ads that you can place on your website. When your website visitors click on any of those links, they will be redirected to Elance. If the traffic you refer posts a job or signs up as a provider, you will receive money for introducing them to Elance.

Referral Program

The Referral Program works much like the Affiliates Program. Hover your mouse over **Resources** in the top main toolbar and click on **Referral Program**. You can also access the Referral Program through the page footer links. For every qualified referral you invite to Elance through Facebook, Twitter, or email, you will receive either $10 or 10 Connects. Also, any contractor you bring will receive 10 Connects as a gift from you.

> **TOP TIPS**
>
> Some contractors may be wondering why they should refer other freelancers to Elance who will eventually become their competitors. However, unless they're designing their business exactly like yours, they most likely won't be direct competition. Writers specialize in different areas and have different strengths and weaknesses. The same goes for programmers, designers, etc. The pool of talent is enormous, as are the jobs to choose from.

We're not talking about making major bucks by bringing in new Elance members. But you can make a bit and help out other people in the process. Have a look and see if it's something you'd like to be involved in.

The Elance University

Within the drop-down menu from the ever-resourceful Resources tab on the main toolbar, click on **Elance University**. This will lead you to several Elance video tutorials. These are great quick references for the basics of making Elance work.

This is another area for you to tap into if you need extra help. The tutorials guide you right through the process as you see it on your screen.

In Summary

By now you should be a virtual expert in how to use Elance. You understand how the system works from both the clients' and the contractors' perspectives, and you know what to do to make yourself stand out.

You've also picked up many tools and techniques for not just winning a few jobs or posting new projects, but taking your online work world experience to a level you may never have expected.

Success stories abound and yours could be next. But you must work smart and hard. You must regularly step back and assess your business and figure out what you can do to take it one notch higher, again and again.

If you follow the guidelines I've presented and diligently apply what fits for your situation, you can succeed beyond your dreams, whatever they may be. From living the freelancer dream life of working at home as your own boss controlling your own schedule, to building your own business more efficiently at a lower cost using talent from around the world. It's all possible and it's already happening every single day.

By reading this book you have a huge head start on your competitors. The rest is up to you. I wish you the best of luck and know you can do it. For questions or comments visit me on my website, www.karenlaceywriter.com.

The Least You Need to Know

- The Elance community contains hundreds of thousands of members and is growing fast.
- The Blog and Water Cooler are excellent resources for new information and to exchange ideas with other Elancers.
- Elance provides you with an independent health insurance resource for U.S.-based contractors and clients.
- You can earn money by referring people to Elance.
- The Elance University is available with short video tutorials.
- You've got a head start already by reading this book—don't stop now!

Glossary

applications These are technical tools specifically designed to help make your virtual office as user-friendly as possible. They include video conferencing, screen sharing, a to-do list, and a service for managing code in a collaborative setting. More applications will be made available in the future.

awarding a job When a client chooses the contractor she wants to hire, she awards the job to him. The contractor is then hired and the Elance virtual office infrastructure and features can be utilized.

bid Much like on eBay, contractors place a dollar bid on jobs posted by clients. The client does not have to take, and doesn't always want to take, the lowest bid. Rather, she awards the job to the contractor of her choice.

category Elance separates contractors into different categories depending on the services they provide. For example, a contractor may be in IT & Programming, or in Writing & Translation. Clients post their jobs within these categories.

client Individuals or businesses that post jobs and hire contractors through Elance.

cloud Business is considered to be conducted in the cloud when files, data, applications, and programs are managed and stored on the internet.

code sharing A way two or more programmers can share the source code they are developing within the same or related projects.

Connects A virtual currency used by Elance. You pay a certain number of them each time you submit a proposal. Each month you are allocated a fixed number of Connects depending on your membership plan.

contractors   Independent individuals and businesses that provide services on Elance. These are the folks that get hired. I also refer to them as freelancers.

Elancer   An Elance client or contractor.

feedback   A written assessment by the client of their work experience with the contractor.

freelancers   Used interchangeably with contractors, these are the people who use Elance to find work.

job post   Also known as a project posting. Each client will post a job on the Elance system that will describe in detail the work that needs to be done. Interested contractors then place bids on these jobs.

keyword   The intuitive word a client will use to search for contractors. Think of when you use Google or some other search engine. The words you type in to start your search are keywords. Elance contractors list keywords that will bring up their profile when clients type the same word(s) in the search box.

level   Refers to a contractor's activity and achievements on Elance. The higher the level, the greater that individual's or business's activity, earnings, and positive feedback.

preferred placement   Also known as a sponsored placement. A feature that highlights your proposal and places it at the top of the client's proposal list. Although preferred placements give you extra visibility, they also cost you more Connects. Three preferred placements are allowed per project posting.

prefunding milestones   Refers to placing funds in escrow before they are due to be paid. This is often done by clients at the beginning of a project.

profile   Each contractor creates a profile that prospective clients view to help determine if they're the best fit for their job. Clients also build profiles, but they're more limited in scope.

proposal   When a contractor places a bid on a job, he will include a written proposal explaining what he will do and why he is the best choice for the job.

ratings   A ranking system Elance clients use to assess work done by a contractor. Ratings are on a scale of 1 to 5, with 5 being the best.

skill tests   Optional tests taken by contractors to rank their skill level in specific subjects against other Elance contractors. Contractors can also choose to self-rate their skill levels.

Tracker and Work View   These work together and are optional on hourly projects. Tracker tracks the amount of time a contractor spends on a specific project. Work View takes random and sporadic shots of the contractor's computer screen and delivers them to the client.

workroom   Each individual job will have a workroom on the Elance system where the client and contractor are able to communicate and manage the project.

workroom messaging   The Elance system that allows clients and contractors to communicate via a message board in each project workroom. All communication here is stored and saved so you can easily refer to it later.

Sample Proposals and Job Postings

Detailed job proposals and postings are at the heart of successful Elancing. While I have outlined which elements are crucial to each in their corresponding chapters, the more real examples you have to work from, the better. Study these and compare them to your own efforts.

Sample Proposals

Here you will find three sample job proposals. Each one is different in style and content, and each one proved successful in the field. I've made comments in bold.

Article Writing

Rachel Ballard is a successful freelance writer on Elance who specializes in health-care marketing, maternal care, pregnancy, and women's health topics. The following proposal scored her not only an article-writing job paying $150 for 500 words, but also a very long-term client relationship. You can find Rachel on Elance at Med4You, and at www.ihealthcommunications.com.

Hello Mascuitto,

First, let me say thank you for the invitation to write for you. My name is Rachel Ballard, and I am a Maternal–Newborn Certified registered nurse, mother, and professional Consumer Health Writer. I specialize in taking complex medical issues (and sometimes those sticky parenting situations) and turning that information into clear, easy-to-read information. Engaging content that is both professional and informative but not stuffy and boring can be hard to grasp—but living it firsthand, and having my medical background, make it easy to overcome.

Here Rachel pointed out the client's needs and explained how they fit her specialty. She also has a friendly, personable style.

I have been assisting breastfeeding mothers (and I nursed myself) for a decade. As a graduate of the University of Louisville's well child program, I have been trained by the best, and had a chance to put that training to work with children of every age.

My research skills are solid—I know which medical journals and websites present accurate data, and which ones to stay away from, so getting correct information will never be a problem here. As a reliable writer, my clients have been happy to have me on board. Working with everyone from private physicians to multi-million-dollar companies makes my background solid.

In the previous paragraph, she listed her credentials and answered the "Why me?" question.

I would love to have the opportunity to work with you and help build the content you are looking for with quality, fun, and informative writing. I am always available for consultation— either by Skype, phone, or email. I do my best to be easy to work with, too—I'm a real girl, doing a great job for my clients.

Great enthusiasm.

One question: what's the turnaround time on this first set of 10 articles? I would be able to have them done within about three weeks, just to give myself time. (I always deliver early, but like to give a window.)

She's asks a relevant question.

Take a look at my feedback comments here—you will see what my clients have had to say about my work.

My bid will be for all 10 articles, for closer to 1,000 words.

Again, thank you for the invitation, and I look forward to working with you soon. Feel free to request writing samples as needed ... I have plenty!

Rachel Ballard, RNC-MNN, BSN
Consumer Health Writer

Website Design

Hi Steve,

This is Raja from WebDesign Solutions. Thank you for taking the time to review our bid! Your project to build a website for your architectural firm is exactly what we do well. At WebDesign Solutions we incorporate a professional team of skilled graphic designers and web developers for exceptional design and development.

Raja addresses the client's specific goal and explains his firm specializes in the solution.

In reply to your concern over the type of website, we recommend using Wordpress as your content management solution. This will allow you to edit or manage your content without the need to know any coding skills.

He answered a question the client had in his posting.

We have a separate team of Wordpress gurus, and our team is 99.9 percent expert in Wordpress solutions. We can customize, rewrite code, design, and do other Wordpress-related services.

STAGE I: Visual design milestone. $420, 7 business days.

The stage will include:

Webpage design (provided as PSD/JPG)

— Homepage mock-up.

— Simple text-based logo can be designed together with a mock-up.

— Up to 3 rounds of revisions based on your feedback.

— Original, unique design for all the deliverables is guaranteed.

— Homepage will be provided as PSD/JPG.

STAGE II: Coding. $500, 8 business days.

The stage will include:

— XHTML/CSS 1.0 transitional, W3C valid, cross-browser, mark-up.

— Light flash effect (3 to 4 rotating images) or music effects are possible.

— Wordpress 3.0 version template creation and configuration to work with approved design. You can familiarize yourself with the system at http://wordpress.org/.

— Uploading up to 6 pages of content. For example: Services, Contact Us, Testimonials, About.

STAGE III: Delivery. $300, 3 business days.

The stage will include:

— Installation of the site on your hosting account.

— Final testing.

— Consultations, explaining how to update the site using Wordpress admin panel, explaining how to create email accounts, etc.

The plan of action is clearly laid out. This amount of detail isn't always necessary, but it worked well here.

We'll expect you to:

— Provide text copy and, if possible, images we can use.

— Fill in our design questionnaire.

— Provide your hosting details (FTP, C-panel).

— Reply to our inquiries shortly. Otherwise it'll be impossible to keep the above-mentioned turnaround time.

What the client is expected to provide is also mentioned. This is a good detail.

Payment terms:

We prefer to work with standard Elance escrow.

Look forward to working with you.

Best regards,

Raja Prasid
Project manager of WebDesign Solutions

Manuscript Editing

This sample proposal is from Cathy Reed, a super-successful Elance writer and editor. You can find her on Elance under the user name Cathy Reed.

Hello,

Thank you very much for the invitation to edit your manuscript. I have edited many books (and also written e-books) on similar topics—leadership, management, change management, communicating change, etc.—and I have an MA in Organization Development. I am inspired by your approach and would love to work on your book.

Cathy begins by stating why she is an expert in achieving the client's goal. She also mentions she's "inspired" by the client's approach. This is both flattering and also means she's paying attention to this specific project.

I have 28 years of experience as a writer, editor, and communications manager and currently edit many nonfiction/business manuscripts and many academic theses, dissertations, and journal articles on a variety of subjects. Where required, I do developmental and structural editing as well as copy editing.

The "Why me?" portion. Short and to the point.

I am bidding $1,400 for the project and suggesting a three-week timeline, but I can vary the time to fit your schedule.

I edit in MS Word Track Changes and am attaching two editing samples from nonfiction manuscripts.

Also, below are testimonials from some of the authors for whom I have edited manuscripts. (You can see many more reviews/testimonials in the Job History and Service Description sections of my Elance profile.)

Please let me know if you have any questions.

Thank you,

Cathy Reed, BA, MA
C. Reed Writing & Editing

TESTIMONIALS

* "Cathy is a phenomenal editor. She is committed to excellence ... provides timely feedback ... is easy to work with. Cathy, you are amazing!" CM

* "Cathy is a superb editor, proofreader, and ghostwriter ... I highly recommend her." PV

* "I could not be happier with Cathy's editing of my book. She showed the utmost respect for my writing style ... I learned a lot from working with her." HE

* "Cathy edited my PhD dissertation. She delivered timely and excellent quality work and provided highly useful comments. I would strongly recommend her for editing other dissertations." AA

Cathy finishes with actual client testimonials. This is a nice touch, and the client immediately sees what others have said about Cathy.

Sample Job Postings

In this section are three sample job postings by clients that show many of the successful techniques I've pointed out. I've made comments in bold.

Website Designed

This sample proposal can be found on Elance's blog in an excellent article titled "Hands-on With the Elance Work System: Part 1," by Matt Katasaros. Not all postings are this detailed, and this is a great example of one that's well done.

> 8-Page Static Corporate Website
>
> **Good, specific title.**
>
> We have a corporate website for a company, Cloud Tele-computers, that needs to be redesigned. The website is currently at www.cloudtelecomputers.com and will remain there for the final site.
>
> **Description of core project goal.**
>
> The site will feature these pages: home, about us, technology, work with us, management/investors, contact, and a demo page. All of the pages (except contact and demo) will be static text/graphic pages with no dynamic content. The contact page will have some static contact info as well as a contact form for users to fill out with questions and comments, etc.
>
> The demo page will need to have a user name/password field that gives the user access to the product demo (which is an interactive flash demo of the product). All of the content (text and graphics) and flash demo will be provided to you for use.

Since the site is so simple, we want to have some added flash features, like button rollover, flash page transitions, etc., to add some sleekness to the look and navigation to the site. These flash extras will be described in more detail to the contractor awarded the job.

The client obviously has a clear idea of what he wants. This is an excellent sign for contractors that this would be an attractive job to have if the price is right.

As per the design of the website, we want something sleek and simple. We really like Apple designs and the Apple website (www.apple.com) and would like to do something loosely based off their site. We have done some sketches to give you an idea of how we would like the site done.

The client has even gone so far as to provide design sketches—a nice big green flag for contractors.

We are on a strict deadline for this job. The job will start the day the contractor is awarded the job and should be completed no later than August 1st.

Thank you.

3D Animation

Effective postings can be written that are much shorter yet still detailed. Following is an example of one such project description. The client's goals are clearly described in a short amount of space, and further information and ideas are available on request. This is well done.

3D Animator for Short Promotional Spot

A clear, detailed title.

We need a 3D animator to animate some graphics for a 30-second promotional spot. The animator will need to create a factory-like setting with a machine at the center of it. The machine is producing robots (very, very simple iconic robots) and sending them down a conveyor belt. Each robot has a unique item on it (i.e., a watch, shoes, etc.). At one point in the spot, the machine will break and start producing the same robots but with an orange stripe across the center of the robot.

This is so well described that you can clearly see what the client is visualizing.

We can provide art direction, designs if needed. Further details can be provided.

And if it's not enough, the client has more.

Virtual Assistant

Full-Time Virtual Assistant

Research, research, research. This is the main aim of this position. You will also be asked to handle administrative tasks in a timely manner, often with fixed and important deadlines.

We are a start-up technology firm specializing in biodegradable plastics. Although we have some steady clients, we are in a high growth phase and need considerable marketing research done. Also, even though we're a small firm, we're very close knit. We'd prefer a trial run of one month to make sure personalities fit.

The client clearly lays out the main goal—research—plus the need to handle extra duties. The purpose of the company is also stated, including the fact they want to make sure everyone gets along. This is a good sign.

Job Description:

Your responsibilities:

— Data analysis/entry into Excel, Word, or other programs
— Research using the internet or other information databases
— Outbound calling to clients, vendors, or others
— Social media and blog management
— Travel planning and coordination
— Email management
— Other miscellaneous tasks that can be performed online
— Must be accessible online and on Elance Work View during agreed-upon office hours

While not warm and fuzzy, the job details are clearly listed.

Your qualifications:

— Previous experience as an administrative assistant preferred
— Broadband internet connection
— Strong understanding of internet and online communication tools
— Ability to multitask and take on multiple projects
— Ability to meet deadlines
— Strong communication skills and attention to detail a must
— A complete Elance profile
— References or an established reputation on Elance preferred

The contractor qualifications are clearly listed.

Index

Numbers

90-10 rule for freelancers, 22

A

Account Manager of team, 101
account types
  basic, 32-33
  business, 34
  individual, 33
accounts
  charges, 33
  fees, 34
  security, 201-202
action plan in proposal, 76
Add to Watch List, 64
administrator of team, 100
advantages of Elance, 42
Affiliates program, 252

agreements
  Elance
    Payroll Services
      Agreement, 200
    Services Agreement
      between Client and
      Contractor, 200
    Terms of Service, 200
  project agreements, 197
    Change Order Agreement,
      199
    Client/Service Contractor
      Agreement, 198
    Detailed Project
      Agreement, 198
    Engagement Letter, 199
    NDAs (nondisclosure
      agreements), 197
    Statement of Work, 198
applications in workroom, 180
Attachments tab (My Jobs), 166
attracting talent
  contractor categories,
    133-134
  projects, 132

P

promotion, 110
communiction, 114
enthusiasm, 113
experience, 112
follow-up, 113-114
profile emphasis, 110-111
talents, 111
proposals, 5, 74
action plan, 76
assessing, 169-170
boilerplate, 169-170
contractor assessment
new contractors, 174
phone interview, 174
questions to ask, 172-173
sample work, 173
contractors, offerings, 75
copy and paste, 78
enthusiasm, 78
genuineness, 75
hiring, 175
ideas for project, 76
incoming, 165
My Jobs page, 167-168
nonproposal proposal, 88-90
numbers submitted, 114
pricing, 82-83
formula, 84-85
negotiating, 85-86
red flags, 85
questions, 76
questions answered, 170
samples, 79-81

spammy, 20
structure, 78-79
submitting, 86-88
understanding of job, 170
unique qualities, 77-78
Public Messages tab (My Jobs),
166

Q

quality, underbidding, 109
questions, in proposals, 76

R

rates, minimum hourly, 47
ratings, 25
profiles, 43
success tips, 230-232
recommendations, 230
red flags
client profiles, 67-68
pricing, 85
Referral Program, 252-253
Refund, Cancel or Dispute
option, 238-241
refunding payment, 239-240
registration
clients, 16-17
Connects, 20
contractors, 17-18

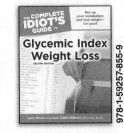

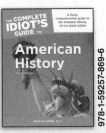
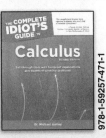
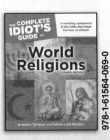

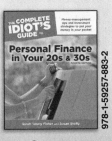
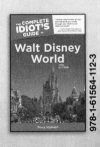